I CLOSE MY EYES IN THE DARK

"Look for the positive in every life situation and often you'll find humor there hiding in the corner"

DENVER E. LONG
BFA MA DPAKR

authorHOUSE®

AuthorHouse™
1663 Liberty Drive
Bloomington, IN 47403
www.authorhouse.com
Phone: 833-262-8899

Published by AuthorHouse 02/01/2022

ISBN: 978-1-6655-4961-5 (sc)
ISBN: 978-1-6655-4960-8 (e)

Contents

Acknowledgment

To my dear wife, Joan C. Johnson-Long,
my *"Jamaican Doll"*, who has been an
inspiration from the moment we met.

"As I watched with curiosity, my mother
placed the delicate little cutting
into a glass of clear water, then she
put the glass in a shady corner
on the window ledge. For days I
watched as the cutting began to
grow tiny roots. The roots grew longer
and longer until they filled
the bottom of the glass, and I wondered silently:
"How did that plant know to do that?""

Introduction

Recently my wife and I were talking about our childhoods and what used to scare us the most as kids. I shared with her that my biggest scare was from a black and white horror movie made in 1942 called _The Beast with Five Fingers_. I saw it in 1950 when I was nine years old. A bunch of us kids would go to the Roosevelt Theatre a couple of blocks away on 15th & Broadway in Gary, Indiana. We usually went on Sundays, after church. We all lived on 15th & Massachusetts, just one block over east and one block south from the theatre. Most of us had some idea what to expect in a movie; the kids who had already seen them provided us with a thumbs up or a thumbs down. Word would spread fast. Westerns were the most popular movies, but they were not scary. Yet nobody had said a word-not a word about _The Beast with Five Fingers_. Not a word. It was as if nobody had seen it. But they had to have seen it because it was on the same matinee program as _Tarzan_, and nobody missed _Tarzan_ movies. Maybe in anticipation of _Tarzan_, they did not pay much attention. My sister, Jo, was one of us. She was ten years old.

The movie starred a creepy, bulging-eyed actor named Peter Lorre. The story was about a series of mysterious murders that appeared to have been committed by a famous dead pianist's severed hand. This all took place at the turn of the 19th century in a small Italian village. The murders had the entire village sheltering in fear. Suspecting that those around him were stealing his money, the famous and wealthy pianist, upon his death severed his hand; it would set out to seek revenge for him. The stage was set when, one night, the occupants of the huge dark forbidding mansion began to hear a piano being played downstairs in the cavernous central parlor. When they looked, there was on one there. One by one the severed hand sought each of them out. One scene changed my life. While lying in bed under a flickering candle, one of the antagonists in the movie thought he felt something moving up the covers on his bed. Ignoring it, he went back to sleep. It was the severed hand that made its way up his leg and over his body to his throat where it strangled the man to death in his bed. That scene scared me more than I realized at the time. It was later that I paid the price for watching it.

One night as I lay in bed, in our dark bedroom, trying to go to sleep, I thought I felt something moving on my bed, but I was way too scared to look. Then I felt something on my foot. There was definitely something on my bed. It was slowly moving up my leg; I froze in terror. When it reached my thigh, I screamed as loud as I could and jumped out of bed. The lights came on and my mother was standing in the doorway trying to figure out what had happened. Sitting on the bedroom floor laughing like a maniac was my sister. Through my tears and trembling voice, I explained that Jo scared me with the crawling hand thing. I was terrified but

Jo was in hysterics, laughing like a madwoman. I vowed that one day she would pay. After my mother reprimanded her, we went back to bed, Jo in hers and me in mine. I did not sleep that night. The very next night I had to go to the bathroom. In the dark I quietly got out of bed walked out of the bedroom, tiptoed around the refrigerator, and went into the bathroom. I flushed and headed back to bed. Just as I was about to step around the refrigerator, out of the dark something gently touched me and whispered, *"Boo!"* My reflects made me yell out loud and swing. There was loud horrifying scream as my mother came running into the kitchen and turned on the lights. Jo was standing there screaming, blood pouring from her nose. After that she stopped with the night pranks.

As I told her the story, my wife she laughed continuously at how much of a 'scaredy-cat'I was when I was a kid. I asked her what she would have done had she been in my position and her answer made me laugh aloud. She said, "I close my eyes in the dark."

Those White Boys

Whenever I meet my wife after work for dinner in downtown Chicago, I always drive the few miles from our south side home to Hyde Park; I park my car and take the *#6 Hyde Park Express* bus to downtown. Non-stop, the bus ride downtown is fast and pleasant. The bus zooms along the mesmerizing scenic lakefront. The bicycle path parallels the expressway all the way downtown. It's a pleasant ride and much less stressful than driving in the heavy downtown traffic. From Hyde Park to downtown is a twenty-minute non-stop ride on Lake Shore Drive. Once that express bus gets onto *"The Drive"* at 47th St, northbound, its next stop is downtown Chicago. The reverse ride is much the same except that it is always dark when we leave downtown heading back south. On most of the late evening and night trips from downtown, the bus gets crowded; it gets 'tight'. My wife and I always get on the bus at the beginning of the route which is near our restaurant. We have open seat options. If you don't get a seat downtown, chances are good that you'll stand all the way to Hyde Park. The riders on the *#6* are from every culture and ethnic group; many live in multi-cultural Hyde Park and in the University of

Chicago campus area where most passengers disembark. It's common to see professors riding alongside students, nurses, teenagers, grannies. Probably half of Hyde Parkers ride the #6-*Downtown Express*.

One night, after my wife and I finished dinner and started to head back south, we got on the *#6* as usual right at the beginning of the route and sat near the front of the bus. We sat in the first row of seats. People began boarding and the bus filled up quickly. At one stop more than a dozen young white men boarded the bus. They looked to be in their early to mid-twenties. About two dozen of them eventually boarded at different stops along the way. The bus was packed. The young men all wore the same uniform: white shirt and bow tie, khaki slacks, and a blue blazer with a pocket hanky. I assumed they were part of a choir or a fraternity. It would have been difficult to ignore them because there were so many of them and they all had to stand up from the front through the full length of the bus. They were tall and blonde. What stood out most about them was that they were all so 'white'- not white like the other white passengers on the bus. You could hear accents in their conversations; it was not English. I thought they might be German. I fought hard with myself to avoid having the word 'Arian' in a negative way, enter my mind. I pushed the thought aside. The young men talked and laughed softly among themselves as they swayed this way and that with the bus's bumps and gyrations. Other passengers smiled and acknowledged them as the bus gained speed.

At one stop, a disheveled black woman got on. She was mumbling incoherently to herself and sporadically

2

cursing loud enough for everyone to hear. She stepped up into the very crowded cabin. She was filthy. And she smelled terrible; we could smell her as she stumbled over passengers. No one wanted to touch her as she ambled her way toward the middle of the bus. People parted as much as the limited space would allow. She was unavoidable, bumping her way through the parade of smartly dressed white boys. She took a high mounted seat that had been quickly sacrificed by a passenger who saw the woman coming. Reeking of alcohol and very shabbily dressed, the woman smelled terrible but worst of all, she got extremely loud and profane. The bus moved along as she continued her vulgar tirade. As the bus gained speed, the woman stunned the entire bus when she suddenly shouted out to the white boys standing along the way and in front of her, some of them eye to eye: *"Hey, white boy, you want some pussy? I got some good pussy! I'll give all ya'll white boys some of this good black pussy!"* The entire bus froze as she continued to harass the nervous young men who were freaking out. But there was nowhere for them to go; they were stuck. They were scared out of their minds. It was a nightmare come to life for them. Some passengers were becoming vocally threatening to the woman. It got so bad that the bus driver shouted out and warned her several times to control herself, but she paid him no heed. Tensions mounted and it got really "tight" on that #6.

I thought how ironic it was that these white guys were packed solidly together like Nordic sardines in a can with nowhere to go carrying a very unpleasant black female sardine as one of their number. She was the sardine that gave the other sardines that smell. The whole situation was extremely uncomfortable and embarrassing for many of the passengers, painful for others. The metaphor I saw was clear and simple. Our lives move along for a limited time on a path of our choosing. We meet people on the ride along the way. Some ride as far as we do. Others get off earlier. Often, we find ourselves in situations that call on us to use every ounce of our wisdom, humanity, and compassion just to survive. We learn that sometimes the best thing to do or say is nothing at all. Those are times when patience becomes the true virtue.

Loud verbal threats were now being hurled at the woman from anxious passengers. The bus driver pulled the bus over at the very last bus stop before the bus got onto the outer drive expressway. Just then a second crowded #6 bus roared up right alongside us and stopped just a few yards ahead. The troupe of terrified young men saw the other #6 and their opportunity to escape. Together, as one, they all frantically bolted, some out the front door and others the rear exit door, hurling profanities back into the bus at the unpleasant woman as they scrambled for that other bus. It was loud and it was ugly, but that other bus was their salvation; they had to catch it. That rear door slammed again and again as they jumped through the two paneled opening, one by one, again screaming back with what could only have been more profanities, all of them running for that other #6. They all boarded that bus as if their lives were in danger. But when they boarded it, they packed it just as they had packed ours, more. They had to stand on that bus, too. Now our bus was less crowded. At the same time our driver got off the bus, walked a few yards away from the bus, pulled out his cell phone and called the authorities for the unruly woman passenger. We could see the bright screen on his phone as he put the phone to his ear. It was dark except for the bus stop shelter. By now our driver had been on the phone long enough for our problem passenger to realize she could be in real trouble if the police came. So, she got up from her seat, cursing, mumbling more profanities, and eventually stumbled to the front of the bus and off. The passengers began to settle down again and get comfortable for the express ride to Hyde Park. Seeing that the woman had gotten off the bus our driver turned and began walking back to our bus to continue our ride. He apologized to the rest of us for the delay and inconvenience but after a several minutes of adjustments, he closed the door and began to pull away from the bus stop. Then it happened. The woman passenger seated near us looked out the front window of our bus and screamed out a shocking message to the rest of us on the bus. Her message shot through our bus like a rocket and the entire bus erupted into loud screams, yells, and hysterical laughter as the message sank in:

"She got on that other bus! She got on the other #6! They're getting on The Drive!!"

The Other Denver Long

I met a teacher and we introduced ourselves to one another. I said, "My name is Denver Long." She responded, "My name is Laurea Doulougeris. It's Greek. You take out the "u" and the "a" in my first name and pronounce it "Lare." We laughed as I stumbled through it. We continued with small talk for a few minutes and then she said, "But guess what! My maiden name is "Long". I responded with surprise. Then she looked at me in amazement and said, "You are simply not going to believe this, but my father's first name is Denver! His full name is Denver Long, too! Is that crazy or what? He's 83 years old and he lives in Colorado!" I responded: "Don't tell me he lives in Denver, Colorado!" We both laughed at the amazing coincidence. He lives in Boulder, Colorado. My curiosity got the better of me and I asked what month Mr. Long was born. It would really be something incredible if he, too were born in December, better yet be a December Capricorn. I was born on December 27th. The other Denver Long was born on January 23rd. Close enough. It seemed ironic that her father was a white man living in Colorado with the name Denver Long and I was a black man living in Chicago with the same name, teaching with his daughter. We were both so surprised at the incident that she asked, excitedly if she could take my picture and send it to her father since they communicate every day. She assured me that her father would be thrilled to the get picture and know that this guy in Chicago had his same name. Since he was older, we agreed to give him that privilege; his name came first. Lare promised to show me pictures of her father and his family. I agreed.

When our paths crossed again, she was excited to show me the pictures of her dad. In one of her photos was a white family of five. The group was outside in front of a small white house. A tall man stood to the left holding a little girl in his arms. Standing next to him was a short stout woman and in front of her were a little boy and a little girl. The man was Denver Long, holding Lare in his arms. The photo was taken in the 50's. Lare giggled with excitement as she talked about the photo and how happy her dad would be to communicate with another Denver Long. With my permission, Lare stepped back and snapped off a couple of pictures of me and sent them off to her dad. She was excited; I was filled with insight, laughing to myself as to how this man was going to react. I doubted that her father in Colorado was going to be excited about a black guy in Chicago with his name–and his daughter. Lare promised to find me as soon as she heard from her dad. I didn't see her the next few days. When we crossed paths again, she seemed a little evasive and, in a hurry, to move along. I asked, "You hear from Mr. Long?" With a short smile and evasive eyes, she responded, "Not yet!", as she scurried away. I do not suppose the Hip Hop pose I adopted in the photo she sent him helped her cause much. It was subtle but it was there, the lowering of one shoulder and the head cocked to the side with me giving the sideways "V" sign. It was clearly a message from the hood. We never heard back from the other Denver Long.

Salt Peanuts, Salt Peanuts*

*(A Tribute to Dizzy Gillespie)

During the holidays, volunteers from different parts of Sierra Leone all came together for celebrations. I was present at a big, lively, 'international' party this time. The party had some local dignitaries and officials, most of whom were there just to get drunk. We were in Kenema where several volunteers lived. Food was being prepared all evening; the smell of the rich, exotic dishes permeated the dense summer air. Delicacies of all kinds were available just for the taking. The music was intoxicating. It was hard to ignore the night's hypnotic and magical atmosphere. To be safe from 'weird', scary foods, and dishes, I decided to stick with the safe salt peanuts that I had lucked-up on. As the party activities increased into the later hours, I explored out back where more festivities were happening. The high life music was simply intoxicating. There was something happening out back that I had not seen before. As I got closer to the large circle of folks in a clearing, surrounded by laughing, jumping, and dancing children, I could see that they were having a blast. A big fire was blazing. The kids were everywhere, all with pales and pans partly filled

11

with water. The children were screaming with delight as they frantically ran around, swatting the air furiously with their hands, filling their pales and pans with the thick cloud of insects that billowed. Then I realized what was happening. A light was shining on a huge termite mound. There were only a few nights in the year that the termites flew out of their mounds to mate. For the termites, it was then or never. As the millions of termites rose from the mound's many openings, the children batted them down into their containers of water, soaking their wings so that they couldn't fly. They jumped up and down, screamed and tussled as they used anything available to swat down as many termites as possible. The bounty would not last all night, so they had to move quickly. Finally, the crush of hyperactivity began slowing down. The children gathered the soaked termites, dripping with water, and spread them all out on paper, allowing excess water to drain. On the fire was a big wok heating up palm oil. When the termites were sufficiently drained and the wok sufficiently hot, cupsful of the insects were put into the hot palm oil. The wok was so hot that there was a huge plumb of steam that rose from it as the delicate wings of the insects were seared off. The termites were stir-fried until golden brown and crunchy. The aroma was enticing. The termites were then poured into paper lined baskets and allowed to drain. Then they were generously salted. I declined several offers from the kids to indulge in the festivities. It was then that I had the epiphany. The termites were the 'salt peanuts' I had been eating all day. One more lesson learned.

The DiNovo Sanction

There were only two African American students in the Industrial Design department of the School of the Art Institute of Chicago when I was a student there from 1963 to 1967. I was one of them. The other student never really seemed focused on school. His attendance was spotty; his design assignments were never in on time. I became convinced of his laxity when he offered to share a joint with me on many occasions. Whenever possible, he would go out into the park and smoke, then come back to class. I always refused. I was twenty-two years old and had never smoked marijuana. In retrospect, it's funny because whenever I went home to Gary and hung out with the guys, we rode around town in a car with the windows rolled up, and filled with smoke, marijuana smoke, but I refused to smoke a joint, for fear of getting high. My buddies laughed hysterically at my naivety. I laughed hysterically, too. I didn't know why. I had never laughed so hard. I was the joke. My ignorance was magnificent.

Eventually the other black student dropped out of school completely. For me, my studies came first. Everything else had to wait its turn. My determination was to be the absolute best I could be. I had dreams to fulfill. I was in my second year of college knowing that the world was out there waiting for me. I couldn't let the world down. It was during this time of self-evaluation and goal setting that I met Kay, a first-year fashion design student who also worked in the administration office. She was short and cute with long silky black hair, sparkling eyes, a beautiful smooth complexion and occupying a body that was simply perfect. She was a doll, full of an energy that you sensed immediately when she was around. She was perfect for me and in my head, I claimed her for myself. One morning, in the cafeteria, I invited her to coffee-she accepted, and our friendship began.

Soon we were having coffee together every morning. It became our routine. I suggested we start flipping coins for morning coffee. She agreed. It wasn't long before we both realized that no matter how the coin was flipped, I won. When she flipped, I won. On some mornings we asked other students to flip the coin for us just to be fair. I still won. It was crazy. Students began betting on who would win and most of the time I won. For most of term it went on like that. It was crazy and the absurdity of it all brought Kay and me closer together. Laughter became our common language. I looked forward to seeing her every morning. She admitted that she looked forward to seeing me, too. It all felt good. It was an exciting time in my life. I was in college. I had a job in the vast underground library of the Art Institute of Chicago, a place most people didn't know existed. And I was working on a degree in Industrial Design, something that had been a dream. The environment was new, the people were new, the languages of intellect and art were new. I was absorbed. The world was waiting for me. Nothing was going to stop me from completing my degree. Death could take a vacation because I would not be available for some time in the future or at least until after these goals were reached. Countless days and nights over weeks, months, years, I spent on the drawing board, rendering, in the library reading book after book, studying, writing, learning, growing, thinking, and focusing. I was crazy focused. The world needed my offerings. Kay was the same way. She was completely absorbed and focused on fashion design and photography. We became good friends mainly because of our mutual respect for each other's work ethic. Neither of us got in the way of the other's studies. She often invited me to her department to watch her work. On those occasions, I didn't talk; I just sat, watched, and listened. She would initiate any conversation. Sometimes the silence would go on for hours. They were golden moments. Other times Kay came to my department and watched me work. Sitting next to me, quietly, as I worked on a rendering, explaining to her what I was working to accomplish in the drawing, she seemed amazed at how a product would slowly appear on the expensive design paper. A couple of the other guys in the department weren't exactly happy about the fact that our relationship had grown so close in such a short time. One student disliked me intensely because, as I learned later, he was hot for Kay.

Eventually Kay and I started dating and then going steady; by the end of the year, we were a couple. Students told us that we looked like the perfect art school couple, always laughing, and having fun. Tears of laughter constantly flowed with Kay and me. We were big fun together. We were just silly and madly in love. Like love stories in the movies, whenever our schedules permitted, we would steal away and spend time, both summer and winter, in Grant Park, across the street from campus. When we were together, nothing else mattered. We both knew, too, without much conversation, that our relationship would end when I graduated. I was scheduled to graduate at least a year before she was and I would be going one way, she the other. We understood that and we were both fine with it; the present was what mattered. Her name was Katherine "Kay" DiNovo. Kay was Italian.

During our years at school, on a few Saturdays, Kay made visits to Gary with me to see my folks and to spend some time away from the hectic school environment. It was quality time. Little did I know the path that our lives would take once Kay met my family. My mother and sister loved her from the very first meeting. It was uncanny the way they all took to one another like they had all been friends before. My sister, Jo, pretended to be amazed at how much Kay liked me. She joked about how any girl could find me attractive. She got vulgar and suggested another reason Kay might find me attractive. We all laughed at that. The three of them, my mother, my sister, and my girlfriend became instant friends. It was very unusual but comforting. My father even coined her nickname; he called her "Shorty". He was well over six feet tall so to him, everybody was short. On that first visit, the three women struck up a conversation that was crazy. Thereafter, whenever they got together and started talking, there was no end to where their conversations would end. They talked about food; they talked about fashion; they talked about personal experiences; they talked about everything. Then the subject of family histories came up and that's when the mysteries of the cosmos began to unfold.

Kay was living in Blue Island with her parents while she was going to school. My mother grew in Blue Island where she attended predominately white, Blue Island Community High School with her older sister, Aisalee, from 1935-1939, the year they both graduated. In those days my mother's name was Irene A. Thomason. Hearing this, Kay shouted out, "My father grew up in Blue Island and graduated from Blue Island Community High School in 1939, too!" My mother asked: "What's your father's name?" Kay said, "Frank, Frank D-i-N-o-v-o". "AAhhhh-h-h! I knew him!", my mother shouted.! "He was the quiet type, and he had a birthmark on the left side of his face", she continued. "I think he was Italian. He didn't like my sister, Aisalee because she always seemed so unfriendly; I think she scared him. Aisalee would just stare at him whenever he came around, so he kept his distance. She even got on my nerves sometimes with that stare of hers. I guess he saw her as my bodyguard." my mother said. She went on to describe him perfectly, right down to the way he blinked when he talked. "That's my father! That's my father!", Kay shouted. "Your father had the hots for me in high school! Your dad wanted to date me in high school!", my mother screamed out. They all screamed and screamed again. My dad came up from downstairs and to make matters even more hysterical, he screamed. It was hilarious. "But you know that wouldn't happen. My folks wouldn't have allowed it back then and you know his family wouldn't have approved", my mother continued. "But he let it be known that he liked me. They all screamed in laughter. "My white father had the hots for my black boyfriend's mother in high school--in 1939!", Kay screamed again. "All the students knew about him, too," my mother continued. Tears were flowing. The three of them couldn't stop laughing and screaming. Kay's father had had a crush on my mother in high school. What were the odds?

Note: My mother and her sister were small and fair-skinned. From their high school photos, they looked almost white. Almost!

Kay's parents, especially her father, never approved of our close relationship. Once they learned that I was black, it was all over. They wanted no part of us. Neither of them had ever met me; neither had ever seen me nor had they ever even spoken to me. Kay's sister, whom I met on one very testy occasion, clearly felt the same way. They heard that my name was Denver, I was black and that was enough. I told Kay that one day I was going to meet her father, look him in the eye and shake his hand, like gentlemen do. She assured me that would never happen. I assured her that it would. Who could have imagined her father wanting to date my mother, a black girl in high school and decades later have a daughter who dates her black son? I figured that if that could happen, anything was possible. Nobody could remain so narrow minded his entire life, I argued. Kay begged to differ with me. She assured me her father would never shake my hand. He had brought his daughters up in a very conservative, Republican, Catholic tradition and was not likely to ever change his views. But now we learn that he had had a thing for my mother, a black girl, in the 1930's. To both Kay and me, it really didn't matter in the least what he thought of our relationship. I was African American; Kay was Italian American. We were happy together and we didn't give a damn what others thought about it. The year was 1965.

THE DATING YEARS

"Make Love, Not War" was the national social anthem. It was a time of war, demonstrations, hallucinogenic drugs, and free love. The Rolling Stones were on top of the music charts with *"I Can't Get No Satisfaction";* it blasted on music systems and radios everywhere. Big social change was in the air and the colleges across the nation were nurturing the angry voices of descent that emanated from students around the nation who opposed the devastating war in Viet Nam. Thousands of young Americans were dying in a land far from home, in a war that they had no part in starting. Rebellion was in the air. America was in turmoil. The Viet Nam War dominated the news. Uncle Sam kept constant vigil on potential recruits, and I kept constant vigil on my selective service status. If you didn't stay in school, you would increase your chances of getting drafted-by tenfold, if you were black. I did whatever necessary to avoid an A-1 status. If I was in school full time and making good grades, I was relatively safe. I lived with the reality that I could easily become draft eligible, but my mind was made up: school or no school, I was not going to Viet Nam.

Living in Chicago, I was the country boy in the big city. I was a design student at arguably the best art school in the country and doing well. What made it even better was that my two best friends who had been attending school before I arrived, both lived in Hyde Park, my fantasy land. Hyde Park was where the action was, and I was in it up to my drawing board. In the 1960's Hyde Park was magical; I was in the center of it, and I loved it. At the Art Institute of Chicago, my two best friends lived in Hyde Park, played musical instruments, were artists and both had white girlfriends. In the artistic/cultural/scholarly atmosphere of Hyde Park it didn't seem to matter. The students came from all over the world to study at the renowned University of Chicago and mixed couples were more common here than anywhere else that I had ever seen. I had to constantly remind myself that I was from Gary, Indiana and hadn't seen much. My two mentors had a magnetism that attracted girls, or maybe it was just the times. Maybe it was just me. And there I was, wide-eyed and anxiously learning how to fit in. The parties were always interracial, and always permeated with the strong, pungent unmistakable smell of marijuana. One party stands out. It was a Halloween party at the University of Chicago that Kay and I attended together. The future would reveal the irony and cosmic forces that prevailed upon me to go to that party dressed as a nerdy Cub Scout. There I stood in long, skinny pants that were way too short for me. They barely reached my ankles. I wore a Cub Scout cap that was a size too small and around my neck I wore the scout scarf, neatly folded, and correctly tied. In the photo, I was saluting either valiantly or comically, depending on how you interpreted it. Next to me stood Kay; she was dressed as my sexy little 'naughty den mother/drill sergeant'. She wore an officer's cap with a fatigue jacket that extended down to her mid thighs. Underneath she was decked out in all black leotards that started at her neck and ended over her toes. The fatigue jacket was kept open for effect. Around her neck, on a long string, hanging to her knees was a plastic whistle, as big as her hand. As the photograph was being taken, we stool there, arms around one another's waists, looking like characters from a Marvel comic book. It was all new for me, having come from across the border from Indiana. I had never smoked marijuana, but it was all around me. I had never dated outside my race, but here I was in an interracial relationship at a great school. It was a wonderful, exciting time.

The University of Chicago was right at the heart of the activities. Some of my academic classes were at the downtown campus; some were in Hyde Park. I was meeting foreign students, graduate students, doctoral candidates, artists of every sort and professors from many disciplines. It seemed that every third person in Hyde Park was somehow affiliated with the university. It was an intellectually stimulating and dynamic environment. It was different; it was exciting. I was going to college, meeting new people from around the world, partying with intellects and artists alike, but most importantly, I was getting an education. Life was good and I was happy. The Denver had arrived.

Kay and I were like two kids when we were able to be together. From time to time we did stupid things at school, just to see what would happen. One time we both sat on the floor, underneath the telephone directory stand that was attached to the telephone booth in the student center. We just sat there, drinking our coffees, peeking out from under the ledge, waving at friends as they walked by. Another time Kay stood right behind me, front to back, body to body, very close and she had me tie a giant bow in the yards of red ribbon that she had wrapped several times around our waists. We were a big present to ourselves. Tears of laugher flowed. The funny thing about our antics was that many students acted like those were the most normal things two people could do together. Some students even told us that together we were making a social statement. We agreed. But the only statements we were conscious of making were those that showed how silly and in love we were. We had crazy fun together. We danced, studied, and laughed together more than most.

Often, we talked about the future and what it held for each of us. From the beginning of our relationship, I had always told Kay that one day she was going to be well-known but jokingly, not too well-known. She was going to be a leader of people, a community leader, and a mother to many, but not too many. I assured her that one day her name would adorn some monument or a building somewhere. She was always moved by my words of encouragement. She was going to be the idol of every little girl in her presence, the envy of every mother she encountered and the wet dream of every teenage boy who saw her, and maybe even a few of their dads. As I expected, she laughed out loud at that idea. We constantly encouraged each other. Other students, mostly fashion design students, were always gathered around her. I often kidded her about what might have happened had her father and my mother gotten together. I suggested that instead of her being my cute, sexy little girlfriend, she'd be my, stupid little sister. My mother even thought that was hilarious. I could see even from her activities in school, that Kay was a leader in the making. Our relationship was pure, wholesome, and good; we made things happen. There were times however, when people outside of the school environment let us know that they didn't really approve of our relationship, but it didn't matter to us.

THE SETUP

Back in the kitchen, the laughter and screaming continued. Jo, Kay, and Mom were having a ball. Then Jo came up with a brilliant, wicked idea. She suggested that Kay take home some of my mother's old high school photographs and let her father 'find' them. It was a devious idea and we all loved it. Once he found the photos, Kay was to ask him about the woman in the pictures to see what he would say or how he would react. His initial reactions would tell her everything. Two of the photos were of my mother when she was sixteen, another at seventeen and one of her in her graduation cap and gown. Kay agreed to do it.

The three of them could hardly contain themselves. Kay, Jo, and Mom were the Three Amigas. The trap was set.

THE STING

Weeks later we were all together again-back in the kitchen. Kay could hardly report her findings because she was laughing so hard. Huddled around her were my mother, my father, my sister, and me tuned into her every word. When she finally got it out; she reported that she 'hid' the pictures at home in plain sight and waited to see what would happen. Her father finally 'discovered' the photos, but he didn't realize that he was being watched. Kay said that when he first looked at the photos, his expression went from curiosity to confusion to panic. From out of nowhere, Kay appeared and when he was asked about the woman in the photos, she said her dad nearly had a 'heart attack'. He didn't realize that Kay had been watching him staring at the photos. Her interrogation had caused him to stutter and fidget. She was having a difficult time getting the details out to us; her laughter interrupted her narrative over and over. Finally, her father said, "She looks like a girl I went to high school with at Blue Island High School. Her name was Aileen or something like that. I think she had a sister, an older sister. They were always together," he added. He was clearly very uncomfortable about the questioning. "Do you remember her?", Kay asked. "Yes, I kinda remember her. Where did these pictures come from? How did they get here?", he asked. "I got them from her, the lady in the photos; her name is Irene Long now. It was Irene Thomason when you were in school", Kay said. He looked confused. "She's Denver's mother!" Not understanding what Kay had just said, "Denver, my boyfriend at school, at the Art Institute, the one you don't approve of me dating. Denver Long, Irene Long, that's his mother you went to school with, and it's rumored that you had a real crush on her at Blue Island High School. Is that true?", she asked. His face went beet red as he avoided eye contact and refused to answer the question directly. Again, she queried him on his relationship with the woman in the photograph. Again, he avoided a direct answer as he began to fidget with the photos in his hands. "She was a nice girl.", he managed to say warmly. Kay knew right then that it was true; her father really had held a crush for my mother back when they were both in high school. He was so busted. We all laughed aloud at the profound irony of the situation. What were the odds of our parents having met and possibly dated when they were in school? It was an incredible series of events that had led to this moment, and it left us all dumbfounded. Yet he, Frank D-i-N-o-v-o, disapproved of my relationship with his daughter.

As it turned out, one week or so after graduating, and saying goodbye to Kay, I was off to see Washington, D. C. to begin training as a Peace Corps Volunteer, final destination-Sierra Leone, West Africa. I would be gone for at least the next two years. The Peace Corps was a ticket to Rome, Italy, my ultimate destination. If I was going to travel, it was going to be now or never. I chose now.

It gets better. Twenty-four years later, in 1989, Blue Island Community High School celebrated its 50ᵗʰ class reunion for the graduating class of 1939, my mother's graduating class. The reunion was held at a country club south of Chicago. My wife, Joan, my sister, Jo, and I escorted my mother to the affair. Other than supporting my mother, I had only one other reason for going to the affair and that was to meet Mr. Frank D-i-N-o-v-o. It was a long shot, but it just might be worth the effort. We arrived early at the venue and found our table. We began to relax and enjoy the music. It wasn't Stevie Wonder, but the music was danceable at times. Passers-by stopped at our table as they recognized my mother and reacquainted themselves. We walked around the huge ball room, escorting my mother as she met more old high school friends and classmates. She introduced us to those classmates she recognized or to those who recognized her. So far, there was no DiNovo. After a while, we returned to our table to continue our celebration. Our table was vibrant, animated, and full of laughter. My mother was having a wonderful time when she suddenly said, "I think I see him." Where?" Jo and I asked in unison. She directed our collective gaze to a table about twenty yards directly ahead of us. A man sat alone at the table. I suggested that my mother not say anything but walk by and make sure it was 'the guy'. She did. It was.

When she returned to our table, I said, "My turn." I left the table and slowly approached the table where the lone man sat. As I got closer, he looked up, smiled and we both spoke. I asked, "Hello, how are you?" "I'm fine, thank you.", he replied. "Are you Mr. DiNovo, Mr. Frank

D-i-N-o-v-o from Blue Island High School?", I asked. He looked at me quizzically, wondering who I was but he responded politely, "Yes, I'm Frank DiNovo, and you are." As I sat down across the table from him, I extended my hand to him and introduced myself as we shook hands. "My name is Denver.", I said. There was silence. He was clearly confused, at first. He had no idea who I was. "My name is Denver Long. You went to school with my mother at Blue Island Community High School.", I added. He relaxed momentarily. "My mother's name is Irene Long; it was Thomason, Irene A. Thomason when you were both in school together. Maybe you remember her. She had an older sister named Aisalee who also went to school with you at Blue Island High School from 1935-1939. My mother and her sister were always together; some thought they were twins.", I added. I could see his mind churning. He was working hard to process the information I was giving him. He listened quietly as I continued. "I went to school, the Art Institute of Chicago with Katherine, Kay, your daughter. It was in the sixties. Isn't that a coincidence?," I said. As I spoke, I reached across the table and spread the photos of my mother out before him. They were the same three pictures that Kay had shown him twenty-four years earlier when she and I were in school and dating. They were the same photos that had nearly given him a 'heart attack' when Kay discovered that he had had a crush on my mother in high school. He squinted at the photos for a moment then reached into his breast pocket and brought out his glasses. He picked up the pictures again and studied them carefully. The transformation on his face began slowly. His face got redder and redder as he flipped through the pictures one by one. He swallowed unconsciously. The memories raced through his mind and exploded into the beet redness of his face as he realized who I was and what was really happening. He looked at me and we stared directly into each other's eyes for an eternity. We said nothing. Then, his eyes told me that he completely understood. I slowly gathered the photos, stood up and reached out my hand again. He didn't get up, but he slowly reached out his hand and we shook again for the second time. He was speechless. "It's been a real pleasure meeting you, Mr. DiNovo," I said sincerely, smiling politely as I turned and walked back to my table.

When I reached my table, I glanced back in his direction and he was still sitting there, motionless, staring at me, stunned. My prediction had come true. I had shaken Mr. DiNovo's hand, twice, something Kay said would never happen. I had earned some real bragging rights and an opportunity to show Kay that, as I had said earlier, nothing was impossible. I intended to brag big time whenever I spoke with her again. She would have to congratulate me on my milestone accomplishment.

THE REUNION

Thirty years had gone by since Kay and I were in school together but from time to time we'd hear from each other. Then in 1994 I got a beautiful card from her. She was living her life as Mrs. Katherine Kay Laube. She had married a photographer, Ed Laube, a white photographer. I know we both chuckled at that. I remember her writing and telling me about him while I was in Sierra Leone. In her letters she related how they had started dating sometime after I graduated and moved overseas. Kay assured me he was a very nice guy who had wanted to date her even before I left the country, but he knew that she was already in a serious relationship with me. She was a fashion designer and photo director, traveling much of the time and working full time with her husband in his commercial photography business. I remembered using her as my model when we were in school, and I was in photography classes. I was happy to know that she was happily married. Included with the card was a beautiful color photograph, taken recently of her two adopted children, a girl and a boy, Mary, and Ed, both Korean. As predicted, she had become a mother to many, but not too many. Her card read:

"Dear Denver,

My folks told me that they ran into you and your family at the class reunion.
I meant to write much sooner than this.
Life is such a whirlwind for us right now. I'm enclosing a photo of our kids. Edmund is10 and Mary is 9. Among other things they keep us really busy these days. My job in commercial photography keeps me traveling out of town about two weeks out of every month.

I'm Chairperson of the Zoning Board in town and am on the board of two other organizations. I can't seem to stop volunteering for things. I guess I feel that life is short and there just isn't enough time to do all the things I would like.

College days at the Art Institute seem so far away now. How are you? What are you doing with your life now? Hope your family is well.

All my best,
Kay DiNovo Laube,
Ed, Edmund and Mary."

Kay knew I would get a laugh out of her Korean kids; that was one reason why she sent me their photo. It was an old joke we shared from school. I had always joked that she would have mixed babies, Italian and black, but mostly black. Our son's name would have been Frank Giuseppe Leroy Michelangelo Mario Jessie Antoine Leon Long. The Frank part would be in honor of her father, Frank. But I knew Mr. DiNovo would always just think of our son as "Booger". Kay's tears flowed like a river when she heard that one. Her laugh was uncontrollable. She laughed a long time about that "Booger" comment. I was happy to receive the card and photo and thought about reaching out and giving her a call. The last time we talked, we ended up in a fit of uncontrollable laughter just like in the old days at school. It took me considerable time, but I finally decided to contact her just to say: *"Hello, Kay and thanks for thinking about me and for sending me the photo of your two absolutely beautiful 'unmixed' children."*

I started with Google, looking for Mrs. Katherine Kay Laube. I learned, to my amazement, that she not only lived in the Fox River Grove area of Illinois, outside of Chicago but that she was, in fact, the Village Board President. I was impressed. I had plenty of ammo to kid her about. I could not wait to let her have it. Her extensive list of personal accomplishments went on: she was the Girl Scout Leader and the Chairperson in both Cub Scouts and Boy Scouts. I was in laugh mode again when I thought about the Halloween party we attended as students, when I was costumed as a nerdy Cub Scout with my 'hot den mother'. I couldn't stop laughing as I read on, remembering what I had said about her being the wet dream of every teenage boy in town, Boy Scout or not, and perhaps a few of their scout dads. I had no doubt that was also true.

To top it all, she was a founding member of the Fox River Grove Lioness Club, and, as I had also predicted, the envy of every mother in town. My crazy predictions were right on the money. Everything that I had kidded her about in school had come true. The final prediction was the one that really blew my mind. The Village planted a tree and placed a boulder with a bronze plaque at its base at Picnic Grove Park Playground and the Lioness Club, which Kay was a founding member, donated two park benches that were also installed at the playground. She got a bronze plaque in a playground. I had predicted a building, but she got a playground. I was still impressed. But I didn't expect:

"Village President Katherine "Kay" Laube passed away suddenly on Monday, September 15, 2008, after a lengthy battle with cancer."

Then, just like the old days back at school, my tears flowed and flowed.

Jonathan Kim

Episode 1: First Encounter

I met Jonathon Kim in 2002 when he was four years old. It was fate-pure and simple. I knew the moment I met Jonathan that he and I were destined to be in each other's lives. He was the happiest, funniest, and most intelligent four-year old I had ever met. He bubbled with energy and curiosity. It was my good fortune and honor to have met Jonathan. Since that day, my life has not been the same.

Seon Kim, Jonathan's mother, owned the Kenwood Cleaners right next door to my American Family Insurance Company office on East 57th Street in Hyde Park, Chicago. She and I became friends soon after I moved into the neighborhood. I began waving at her every morning as I passed her window on my way to my office. She always smiled and waved back. One morning I decided to stop in and introduce myself. Seon, a Korean, was a tiny attractive woman who I imagined was in her late twenties or early thirties. Her manner was gentle, and she often laughed easily when I made a silly comment. Her space was neat, clean, and pleasant. I realized right away that she had difficulty speaking English easily. She often apologized for not being able to say exactly what she wanted to say but I dismissed her frustrations and helped her with whatever it was that she was trying to tell me. In time our communication got better and better. I thought Seon was a sweetheart right from the beginning. We were neighbors and I liked her a lot. One morning I bought Seon and myself coffee and before long that was our regular routine, some days she treated; other days I treated.

One morning, as I passed her shop and waved, I saw a little boy sitting on the counter. He seemed a bit puzzled by my waving gesture, not knowing if or why I was directing my attention to him. He waved back at me, and I waved again. After I opened my office, I went back to Seon's window and looked in. He was still sitting on the counter, so I went in. Seon said, "Dember, this is my son, Jonathan. Jonathan, this is Mr. Dember, our next-door neighbor." I said, "Hi, Jonathan." "Hi, Mr. Denver. You got a funny name, Denver", he responded, pronouncing my name perfectly. He spoke both English and Korean. There wasn't the slightest hint of a Korean accent; his English was perfect. I asked Seon if his Korean had an English accent, and she said his Korean had no accent. Jonathan spoke with a clarity that caught my attention right away. He was funny, friendly, and very curious about me, the black guy next door. He wanted to know everything about me, right then. I decided to take his picture, so I asked Seon if it was ok. She said it would fine to take his picture, so I ran back to my office and got my digital camera. When I returned, Jonathan was sitting on a high stool behind the counter as though he worked there, his little white undershirt emblazoned with a picture of a wicker basket filled with puppies. To complete his little outfit, he sported blue and white striped shorts. In one hand he held the telephone and with the other, he dialed. He was laughing and making ridiculous funny faces at me as I began snapping pictures. Seon, noticing my concern about his handling of the phone, assured me that he was not playing with the phone; he was calling his maternal grandfather--in Korea! After a few minutes of dialing and waiting, Jonathon broke into a happy laugh as he began speaking in what seemed to me very rapid Korean. I was amazed. As he spoke, he became ridiculously animated, gesturing to me as though he were a karate expert, holding the phone in one hand then the other and thrusting his other arm at me in threatening poses. I continued snapping pictures. One after another, he continued making different gestures with his free arm, causing me to laugh as I snapped shot after shot. Seon laughed too as she stood looking at Jonathan and me engaged in a two-party comic drama. Still in doubt about his conversation, I jokingly told Jonathan to tell his grandfather that I said hello. Without the slightest hesitation, he blurted out something in Korean in the middle of which I heard "Denver" as he broke into hysterical laughter. Then he said my name again and again as though he and his grandfather were sharing a laugh at my expense. I was clearly the butt of the joke. Jonathan had already impressed me-a lot!

Jonathan usually visited his mother's shop on Saturdays when he rode in with her from the suburbs. His father, David, worked on Saturdays. As the weeks passed, Seon and I continued our morning coffee ritual and laughed about my first encounter with Jonathan. She said that Jonathan told her that he liked me because I was silly. I took that as a compliment. One morning, as I stepped into the cleaners to greet Jonathan and Seon, she announced that Jonathan was treating me to coffee. He had the money, and he was going to take me to The Medici and buy the coffee. I accepted the offer and off we went to begin a brand-new friendship and adventure together. I had known him for about two months and now he was away from his mother with me, out of her sight. I felt good knowing that she trusted me enough to let me take her four-year-old away from her on an errand. Seon's little shop was only a few doors down from The Medici Café where we got our coffee every morning but still it showed tremendous trust. Instinctively I held onto Jonathan's hand as we left the cleaners and proceeded down the street. As we approached the busy alleyway which divided the block in half, I gave Jonathan's hand a gentle squeeze as I came to an abrupt complete stop. He looked up at me quizzically, wondering why we had stopped so suddenly. I pointed out to him that we must always stop and look down the alley before we crossed to the other side. "Never, ever run across the alley without stopping to check for cars", I said. Asked if he understood, he gave me a broad smile and a hearty nod. Together we looked down the alley to make sure no cars were coming then we continued our journey. At that moment I looked back to see Seon standing outside the doorway of the cleaners with a big smile on her face. I released Jonathan's hand as soon as we crossed the alley, and he took off running for the front door of the cafe. We were about to become *"Legends of East 57th Street"*.

What Dreams Are Made Of

I decided to join the Peace Corps while I was in college. It offered travel and adventure and to me, that combination was irresistible. As a kid, I fantasized about living in foreign lands with all kinds of people, eating new foods and learning new cultures; it meant taking risks that I would not have normally taken. It was all about adventure. Early on, most of my time was spent in my head. The pictures in my books fired me up. It was easy to just stare at a photograph and find myself in the photo strolling along some cobblestone street like it was my neighborhood. To follow my heart wherever it led me was my determination. Rome, Italy was my goal and the Peace Corps turned out to be my ticket to cross the big pond. I was going to Rome, no matter what.

Girls were gaining a higher priority in my life, too. I imagined myself falling in love at first sight with worldly beauties and eloping, riding off into the sunset on a black stallion. I'd have wild, romantic flings, adventurous escapades of folly and romance with capes, candles, and confetti. My fantastical adventures covered Europe, Scandinavia and time permitting, Asia. I loved French,

Belgian, German girls, girls from Africa, Japan, Korea, Sweden, I loved them all. By the time I was twelve years old, I wanted beautiful girls from exotic places around the globe to find me completely irresistible. Some would argue which one of them would take me home with them. I'd always give in to one or the other girl, feigning resistance, sometimes encourage one girl to bring along the other girl. They would all want me forever and they would agonize about my eventual departure. They would all know that I'd have to return to my vast kingdom far away in the West across the great ocean, on the other side of the world. In my mind there was room for all of them. There was a lot going in my heart and in my head.

The aroma of freshly baked bread wafted through the warm morning air as I strolled the streets of Paris, along the Champs-Elysees greeting people. "Bonjour! Bonjour!" the girls would all smile at me as I passed. I'd take pictures with several French girls at the Arche de Triumph and more pictures at lunch. One famous very chic restaurant we favored was the L'Astrance. Eloquent; my French was perfect. The girls never paid for anything: I was their special guest from America, and I would spoil them with my vast wealth. It was the same in Rome. Girls were everywhere and they all wanted me. But my real goal in Rome was the Coliseum. With any luck I would even get to meet a few gladiators. The world was mine to imagine as I chose. If it didn't exist in my head, then it didn't exist, and my room was where it all happened. My room was as vast as the universe. There was no place I couldn't go, no wonder I couldn't see, nothing I couldn't do and no person in the world, living or dead that I couldn't meet and talk to-in my room. Thanks to my wall maps, encyclopedias and books, learning was fun and exciting. My super set of American College Encyclopedias and dictionary was my magic carpet that would transport me anywhere in the cosmos. Sometimes when I felt enthusiastic about learning something new, I'd pick a volume of the encyclopedia set and randomly open it to any page. Whatever was on that page, like it or not, was what I read and studied for that day. Every day I went on romantic/intellectual/creative journeys into my mind; each journey better than the previous one. What was a mind for if not to use it to change the world for the better? I was on my way.

My mind was made up. I was determined to get to Rome if I had to walk to the east coast of the United States and back stroke across the Atlantic Ocean. Fortunately, I didn't have to do that because my junior year in college was when Peace Corps recruiters came to my campus looking for new volunteers. I made no immediate connection with being a volunteer in West Africa and Rome. It didn't occur to me until after I had completed an application. The program slipped my mind until a letter from the government came, informing me that I had been accepted into the U.S. Peace Corps. It turned out that my assignment was Union Teachers College in Bunumbu-Sierra Leone, West Africa. I would be the official head of the Art Department in addition to teaching English, Social Studies, History, and anything else I had in my "portfolio". I'd be teaching everything. I looked forward to the challenges and opportunities it offered me, not to mention all the girls I was going to meet. One week after graduation, degree in hand, I was off to Washington, D.C. to begin U.S. Peace Corps training. Most of the trainees taught in the high schools during the summer session. Then we attended language lessons as we got our shots and physical checkups. We left D.C. at the beginning of July, headed for the Caribbean islands.

JSA: JAMAICA SCHOOL OF AGRICULTURE

At the end of July, we trainees left the farm fields at the Jamaica School of Agriculture in Spanishtown, Jamaica to complete the next leg of the training. All summer, during every phase of the training, we practiced the African languages we'd be using when we arrived overseas. The Jamaica training taught us an enormous amount about agriculture; it also gave us stamina as farmers since some of the group would be farming when they reached their assignments upcountry. We were being shown what it would be like living in the bush. The last stop in the program was Trinidad and Tobago. After the Trinidad phase, we had to decide to go forward or to go home. Many volunteers by now were experiencing all sorts of physical ailments. The change in diet and daily routine had taken its toll on all of us. A couple of volunteers go so sick that they had to be sent back home for treatment, ending their training. My stomach began to ache, and I was developing hemorrhoids. I was getting more miserable by the day. The thought of getting on a plane heading in the opposite direction of home and comfort didn't ease my suffering.

LUCY IN THE SKY WITH DIAMONDS

Lucianne (*Lucy Anne*) Powell was a striking redhead California trainee who caught my eye the first time I saw her in Jamaica during the training. She was a picture of health and youthful beauty, and I wanted her bad. She was hot! Whenever there was a big meeting on campus, she somehow ended up sitting, or standing near me. Or it was me always getting closer to her. We had good, strong positive vibes and I liked her. Being the eternal optimist, I thought or hoped she felt the same. She even told me once that she thought I was smart and funny. My response was that I thought she was hot! We enjoyed each other's company whenever a few minutes of spare time allowed us to be close. Our conversations never lasted more than a few minutes, she was usually heading in one direction on campus and me in another. Lucianne was slender and vibrant with beautiful legs that I noticed immediately. Her hair was very short, curly, and flaming red. Freckles filled her face; they sparkled in the bright warm sunlight. She reminded me of the little Annie character. Whenever I was around her, I fantasized about her bush. I imagined it was soft, lush, and red.

Lucy was exactly my height minus the wedge heel shoes she always wore. I loved the way she always smelled fresh and minty. Did I say, she was hot? I was drawn to her heat: *"Punish me with your hot body! Make it hurt so good! Spare me not the lust!"* It was difficult to stay focused when I was near her. More than once, she stared directly at me just as I was having a real kinky thought about her. It was like she was reading my mind, like she knew exactly what I was thinking or what nasty thing I was doing to her in my head. Whenever that happened and it happened more than once, she always smiled at me which only made it worse. It was like she was enjoying it. I never said a word out of line to her, but my bulge and heavy breathing gave me away. Our schedules kept us busy during most days and evenings. Whenever there were a few hours of freedom, everybody was usually too tired to get active again-especially on weekends. There was very little leisure time. Lucy and I continued to smile at one another whenever our paths crossed on the sprawling campus. Despite my constant and growing hemorrhoidal agony all I could see in my mind was Lucianne-naked. In my favorite fantasy she'd come to my door, and I'd invite her in. I'd close the door behind us. From across the room, she'd turn and start to strip, approaching me as her flimsy dress piled up at her feet. Her panties would fall to the floor. And there it would be-the red bush of dreams! The closer we got the hotter we became. Her hands would slowly caress her smooth, delicate body as she gyrated closer and closer to me. Having dropped my shorts and underwear, my erection would cause her to gasp. She'd reach out to touch me and I'd– wake up!

Of all the trainees travelling in our group somehow Lucianne and I flew together from Montego Bay, Jamaica to San Juan, Puerto Rico and then on to Port of Spain in Trinidad. How that happened is a mystery. We became travelling buddies. Lucianne was an unknowing comfort to me during my painful travels. She had no idea of my constant agony. There was also the challenge of fighting off the effects of the numerous immunization shots we all received. I was twenty-five years old, fresh out of college with the world at my feet. It was an exciting time; We were travelling, meeting new people, seeing new places, flying everywhere and even learning new languages. The whole world was wide open for me. Adventure was my driving force and it hung heavy in the air but after a month of training on the island, I left Jamaica with a Lucy on mind, and a pain in my ass. I was miserable.

UNIVERSITY OF THE WEST INDIES - TRINIDAD & TOBAGO

Some of our initial training group had already been training in Puerto Rico but they didn't get to see Jamaica. My group saw both. From Puerto Rico, everybody headed for Port of Spain, the capital of Trinidad and Tobago, commonly known as 'the true Caribbean' because the island is only seven miles off the northeast coast of Venezuela. It's true South America. Our remaining weeks of training were at the University of the West Indies in St. Augustine, one of the four campuses of the University. The *St. Augustine* campus opened in 1960, the year I graduated from high school. The first campus, the *University College* was established in 1948 in Mona, Jamaica. And in 1962 the *Cave Hill* campus was established in Barbados. The campus was sprawling, laid out across a luscious green landscape. The weather was always perfect, and the sun shone brightly every day as the soft breezes swept across the campus from the sea. We trainees worked daily to refine our language, social and teaching skills. It was during our stay in Trinidad that many of the trainees were afflicted with dysentery and all sorts of tropical ailments. For days many of us were unable to do anything but stay close to our dorm rooms and wait it out.

During the training, we had situations with new instructors whom we had not met previously in the program and who all spoke Mende, Temne and Krio, languages we all had to learn to be effective communicators while in the bush. None of the languages were written; they were all verbal. Though English was the official language of Sierra Leone, the students at Union College where I was going, were from different tribes and spoke one or more languages. A third of the population spoke Mende; nearly a quarter spoke Temne but about ninety percent of the population spoke Krio, a mixture of English and various indigenous languages. You could get by anywhere in the country if you spoke Krio, so emphasis was placed on it. We were judged by the fluency and use of intonations that we had developed. Some situations could be lifesaving, depending on one's abilities to communicate. The proficient volunteers learned all three languages. Lucianne was one of them. Mende was my challenge. The weeks that followed were filled with more language classes and field work, learning how to grow vegetables and live off the land. The days were filled with manual labor duties; the evenings were filled with classes. It was a grueling schedule. One focus of the training was to ensure that everybody was physically and emotionally fit to take on the challenges. On weekends we all just crashed. That was what I did on weekend mornings

By the end September the training programs were about finished, and again, it was time to head either overseas or back home. It was time to make that final decision. Some trainees changed their minds at the last minute and abandoned the program. It was a tense time for many. It was made clear to us at the end of the training that once we boarded that plane and took off, there was no turning around. Those with the courage to take on the challenge excitedly chose to move forward. I was one of those. If I could leave home and the country with two quarters in my pocket as I had done and get as far as Trinidad, I was good to go. Leaving home for Africa for at least two years was quite a decision to make but my mind was made up, I was moving forward-hemorrhoids or no hemorrhoids.

It was unusual for someone to be knocking on my dorm door at seven thirty on a Sunday morning. I was in pain, and it annoyed the hell out of me. Everybody on campus must still be asleep yet there was one person who found it necessary to be knocking on my goddamn door. I was not sleep but neither was I fully awake. I heard the rapid taps at the door which I tried hard to ignore. Again, and again the door tapping continued. In agonizing pain, I dragged myself towards the sound of the annoying sound, wondering who could be so inconsiderate. My hemorrhoid condition was now at critical level. My agony had spilled over into my attitude and behavior because I was really pissed at whomever it was knocking on my door at this hour. It had been to my benefit that the past two days had allowed me to remain lying in my bed, in relative darkness not having to move. Just the thought of walking was agonizing.

I opened the door to the blinding glare of sunlight that poured down. At first, I couldn't tell who it was standing in front of me. It was a girl. Her body blocked the sunlight as she stood there in complete shadow. When I looked harder at her, I could see that she was smiling. She was standing in my doorway and dangling from her hand was what I initially thought was her handkerchief. I was wrong. They were panties, pink panties. In a flash, before I could react, her other hand dropped to the hem of her tiny pink cotton dress and lifted it way above her waist, exposing her entire body. She was stark naked. Her two pink nipples smiled at me as the dress exposed them to my frenzied frantic gaze. It was the most beautiful slender body in the world, a magnificent ivory sculpture. I unconsciously looked down between her thighs and there it was - a bush that dreams are made of. It was the kind of bush I had dreamt of meeting and introducing myself to someday. That day had obviously come, and that glistening bush literally came to my door. It all happened in a flash. I fought hard to maintain my composure, but the bush got bigger and brighter. I was mesmerized, as it spoke to me. Suddenly with just a slight movement, she parted her legs just enough to make me gasp aloud. The bush stared at me; I stared back. With a soft smile on her face, she leaned forward and said, "Good morning! Can I come in?", Luci said as she kissed me on the cheek, pulling her dress up over her head as she skipped pass me and stepped inside.

Snapshots from the Dark Side

The first time I was a patient in a hospital was when I born; the second time was when I got circumcised. It's like it was yesterday. I was three or four years old, pass the time the procedure should have been done, but it was better late than never. When I close my eyes, I can still smell the ether fumes that permeated the hospital corridors. It was a sickening smell that clung to your clothes and seemed to remain in your nostrils. But as nauseating as it was, it did the job of putting you to sleep. My experience took place at Methodist Hospital in Gary, Indiana. I remember spending what seemed like forever in a big, cold, dark room, alone, waiting for my mother to come and get me. I awoke bandaged, hurting, and scared. The slats of my crib created a cell that imprisoned me. I was a helpless prisoner still nauseous from the ether fumes. I was a prisoner with my ding-a-ling in a sling. I imagine that I looked like I had a hotdog between my legs with the bandages serving as a bun. I was four years old, but already life was proving to be difficult. I just wanted somebody, anybody, to come and keep me company or better yet just take me home. Someone heard my call. She was big, ashy, ugly, and white.

If there was a hell, I had just entered it because she was obviously the *Demon Nurse from Hell.* She was ten feet tall with stringy, washed-out blonde hair that extended down below her nurse's cap; they looked like that of the Medusa. She was a ghost; and I could smell her foul breath from a distance as she came closer to my little enclosure. Her red eyes glowed in the dark as she approached. Her nostrils flared wide. She had paper-thin lips. The thin slash that was her mouth resembled a horizontal gash across her lower face. A couple of thick, black hairs sprouted from her chin. She wore a starched nurse's uniform and, her white cap resembled two horns, the tips so sharp they could have punctured the skin. She was the devil's girlfriend, and I was terrified. Though her conversation was short and to the point, I could smell her foul breath as she shouted out: "Be quiet!" By comparison the ether was beginning to smell pretty good. I went into a blind rage and screamed at the top of voice. She was not deterred. In one swift, arching motion, she was lifting me up, tilting me backwards, off my feet and back down into the crib, on my back. As I lay there helpless, furious, and screaming, I scanned my limited vocabulary for words, any words that could express the fear and loathing that I felt for this hideous creature that was intimidating me. Nothing came to me. As hard as I tried, I couldn't think of any words to describe the horrible monster. I cried myself to sleep, hating my keeper. I awoke even more furious for having fallen asleep. Years later, I realized that the word I needed but had no access to at the time was *"Bitch!"*.

It has been over sixty years since that encounter with the *Demon Nurse from Hell.* Much has changed over the decades. This time it was more curiosity than nervousness that overwhelmed me as I lay on the clean hospital bed. I was an adult now and not afraid of a big, bad, blonde bully bitch. In fact, my current nurse was a small, very attractive young chocolate-black woman who attended to me; she was a real cutie-pie. She kept referring to me as Mr. Long. I said warmly and a bit suggestively to her, "Just call me *"DenDen""*. She laughed out loud and said, "Ok, Mr. Long." Her smile was warm and genuine; her white stockings were a real turn on. I noticed when she turned to walk out, her manner made me feel comfortable and at ease and a little horny. She wore a colorful uniform that modern-day nurses wear. Her outfit didn't have the formality of the old-fashioned dagger tipped cap. In short, she was hot. What hadn't changed was the lack of privacy that we are so used to owning. One learns humility at the hospital, especially men. Egos and pride are left at the front desk, as it should be. But sex remains in the back of men's' minds. The irony and funny thing is that two conflicting emotions are in play at same time. Your ass is out but you want to keep your genitals covered.

A KODAK MOMENT

The week before, while having my regular physical checkup, my doctor suggested that it might be a good idea for me to also have a colonoscopy. My brain began to race, figuring out what the term meant without appearing ignorant to the doctor. I knew what the colon was and what it did. I also knew that 'scopy' meant to view or examine. So, she wanted me to have my colon examined just like men should have their prostates examined. No problem! Knowing what the colon was, I wondered how they'd get to it. It had never occurred to me how the colon examination was to be done. I had had rectal exams before, and they were nothing to get anxious about; all it took was a good finger, a few minutes and it was done. I also knew that most men never talked about that because it was a sensitive subject and a 'man thang'. Men don't like to discuss what doctors do with their fingers when they examine for prostate problems. A finger can be a most unpleasant and intimidating appendage when used properly. Asked if I had ever had a colonoscopy, I paused and said, "I don't think so." She chuckled and quickly assured me that if I had ever had one, I would remember it. That was not comforting to hear. Her response left me a little anxious. Under my breath I thought: "If you've had one finger, you've had 'em all. She explained that the examination was a routine procedure and went on to say that, like women getting pap smears or mammograms on a regular basis, men should have the procedure done every few years or so just to be safe. I told her that I understood, and it sounded reasonable to me. So, I made an appointment to have the procedure done. As we continued with the physical examination, she reported to me that my heart sounded strong, my lungs were clear, and everything was in good shape. But when she began to give me the rectal exam, it dawned on me that if the procedure was so routine and simple, why didn't she just do it then while her finger was in play. That's when she explained that she didn't do the procedure because it was one in which doctors had to sedate me and insert a camera into me rectum to take pictures and examine the colon. I laughed at first, then gasped and said, "A camera!" My mind immediately flashed. All I could think of at that moment was my 35mm reflex Pentax. "Doc, tell me you're kidding." She was not kidding. That's when it all became clear to me. No wonder she said that if I had ever had one before, I would certainly remember it. I would also probably have had the pictures framed. Just the thought was enough to bring dismay. Despite the cold sweat that ran down my back, I could not help but think what good comedy material it would be, especially if it were somebody else. "It's gonna be a Kodak moment," I thought. "Need prints?" The joke potential seemed endless. Would it be proper to call these pictures "portraits" or "landscapes"? I was on a roll. And then think of the doctor's point of view. What a job. Would it be proper to call that doctor a photographer? I was laughing so much that my doctor, who looked younger than some of my underwear, began laughing with me. She said she loved my sense of humor and told me that I would have no trouble with the procedure. I told her it was easy enough for her say but when was the last time someone had put a camera up "there" and taken pictures? With this, she almost lost her composure. With tears in her eyes, she maintained her cool long enough to write me out a prescription and give me the colonoscopy preparation instructions. We both laughed but for very different reasons. She gave me a prescription to be filled and written instructions to follow; they seemed simple enough. I was to stay home from work the day before the procedure and I was not to eat anything at all; I could only drink clear liquids. That made sense. At 9:00 a.m. on the day before the procedure I was supposed to drink a ten-ounce bottle of Citrate of Magnesium. That was to get the show started. I remembered Citrate of Magnesium from childhood at home when my mother kept a bottle in the refrigerator. I remembered the lemony taste of the laxative. As a kid, I liked it. That part was easy. At 5:00 p.m. after the Citrate had done its work, I was to begin drinking what the prescription called GoLytely (go-lightly), the four-liter container of industrial strength laxative that I was supposed to mix with water. I was to drink an eight-ounce glass of the stuff every ten minutes. Every ten minutes! The doctor made it clear that I was not supposed to sip it but drink the whole glass down at once and continue the procedure all evening until the entire container of solution was gone. After about three hours of that, the solution began going right through. I was 'going lightly'. But I had a quarter container left and four more hours to go. By midnight I had consumed most of the solution and felt emptier inside than I ever knew possible. Before I retired for the night, I finished off the remainder of the liquid. I went to bed satisfied with myself for having followed the instructions to the letter.

The next morning, Joan, my wife, accompanied me to the hospital. It was mandatory that I have someone with me to drive me home since the procedure required my sedation. The hospital had made it clear that without a person to drive me home, the procedure would not be performed because of the liability exposure due to the sedation. Technically, the sedative would not completely wear off for twenty-four hours. We arrived around 8:45 a.m. at the brand-new wing of the hospital. I was in good spirits. I was told that we should be completely done and out of the hospital by noon or one o'clock at the latest, allowing approximately one hour for the preparation, another hour or so for the procedure and another for the sedative to start wearing off. They had scheduled me for 9:00 a.m. and no sooner had I signed in at the desk than a nurse came out and escorted me through some doors to another section of the floor. The sign read: Gastrointestinal Procedures. Little did I understand at that moment how accurate that sign was.

The nurse stopped at one of the cubicles, invited me in and instructed me to disrobe down to my underwear, put on one of those infamous ass-out hospital gowns and relax on the bed. She said it was fine if I left my undershirt on since it was very cool in the hospital. She pulled the curtain behind her as she left the cubicle. Mumbling to myself, I finished disrobing, put on the gown as she had instructed, sat on the bed, and waited for the next step. After only a few minutes the nurse returned with a clipboard and began asking me a series of routine questions about any allergies, medications, or ailments. When she finished asking the questions, she began preparing an IV, at the same time she explained to me what would happen during the procedure. She assured me that it would not be painful or even uncomfortable since I'd be in a 'dreamlike' state. She said that during the procedure, air would be blown into my intestines and colon to inflate them to make the procedure possible. Air! First a camera! Now air! What next popcorn! I had heard about 'blowing smoke', but air! Probably cold air.

When I was all prepped, I pulled the sheet over me; the nurse pulled back the curtain of the cubicle and had me lie down on a gurney as she wheeled me down the short, bright, sterile corridor. I was wide awake and trying to take in all the sights in my line of vision as she negotiated the corner at the end of the corridor and into a small surgical procedures room. The room was about twenty feet square, sterile and filled with equipment. The room was very cold. Everything in the tiny room looked new. It was no wonder, the entire building and complex had just recently been completed, and I remembered how different the hospital was from the dark, musty corridors of Methodist Hospital in Gary and the *Demon Nurse from Hell* from my childhood. I was at the University of Chicago where they say some of the brightest minds in medicine practice medicine. I hoped that was true because every doctor I saw that day, looked like they had just graduated from middle school.

The monitor over my head and to my left showed some charts and graphs; it also had my name displayed in the upper left corner of its screen. My eyes glanced from one side of the room to the other, taking in all the intriguing instruments and machinery; I was fascinated with it all. I even wondered aloud what each piece was used for. I wondered about the camera but refused to ask for fear that seeing it would ruin my day. The nurse then said good-bye and quickly turned and left the room. I hated to see her go; she had been so pleasant, and we had had a few good laughs together. My attention was abruptly averted as, what

I thought were ice packs, were placed under the sheet and on my abdomen. I screamed like a little girl. The doctor had caught me off guard and was examining my midsection for whatever they examine it for. She wore rubber gloves, even so, her hands were as cold as ice, and she laughed out loud as I nearly jumped off the table. She apologized, laughed again, then pulled my undershirt down and continued the cursory examination. She was a cutie-pie, too. The doctor was a tiny very attractive young Asian woman. That was just great, I thought! The doctor introduced herself to me and explained to me exactly what was going to happen during the procedure. I was fascinated by her, who, again, looked as though she had just gotten old enough to get a driver's license. She seemed barely as tall as the bed I was lying on. But her demeanor was very professional as she adjusted her wrinkled, green surgical gown and stretched another pair of rubber glove over the pair she was already wearing. We laughed when I asked why two pairs of gloves and she responded to my surprise with: "My hands are cold". I asked questions about the procedure; she asked questions about me. As a matter of formality, she held a form before me to read. The form required my signature before any sedatives could be administered. I read over the form and signed it; I continued to ask questions. To my surprise and delight the doctor continued to answer every question I put to her, indulging me, thinking that I was scared. I was completely at ease and not the least bit nervous; curiosity was more my state of mind. She assured me that the procedure I was about to undergo was routine and it would only last about forty-five minutes to an hour, time that I wouldn't remember since the sedatives would eliminate any such memory. I doubted that but I kept the thought to myself. As the other doctor prepared the sedative and approached me, I suddenly became aware of the IV I had been given before I was wheeled into the small room. It had been done so precisely that I had nearly forgotten about it. I asked the doctor what kind of sedative was being administered for the procedure. The answer was Demerol and Valium. Why Demerol and Valium? She explained that it was a combination of pain killer (Demerol) and sedative (Valium). As foolish as it seemed, my mind swerved around the question of whether they would give me enough medication to eliminate any pain or better yet, to make me unconscious. The doctor said it was time for me to be sedated and she inserted a small syringe of sedative to the IV in my arm. At the same time, she introduced me to another doctor, a male doctor, who was just entering the room and who would be assisting. He introduced himself and we made small talk as my questions continued. She pushed a small plunder down and I watched the solution slowly flow into my IV. The male doctor asked if I felt drowsy yet. I said "No, not yet". Then I asked how they would know when I had had enough sedative since I would still be awake and in what they called a 'dreamlike' state. Not fully understanding what the procedure included, I felt that there was probably not enough sedative in the building to do the job effectively. He laughed and assured me that when I had enough, I would certainly not be asking any more questions. We laughed and at the same time I raised my head and responded quickly with: "Well, Doc, I think maybe you should do me again because I'm still awake and kicking. My head landed back on the table with a soft thump. There was no gradual fading away, no slow darkening of my senses, no loss of coherence; there was no music and nothing that resembled a transition from state to another. There were no rainbows of spiraling colors to temp me into oblivion. There was no euphoria, no voice calling me into the great void of unconsciousness. There was no dreaming, no floating off into space; there was nothing. A little concerned, I asked, "Doc, how long is it going to take befor.................."

It was instant and complete. One moment I was wide awake, the next instant I was out cold. My consciousness had abandoned me in mid-sentence. I was out like the proverbial light, completely unplugged. When my eyes began to open, I was in the little cubicle; Joan was sitting next to the bed. "How much longer before the procedure?", I asked. Laughing softly, Joan said, "It's over". I was back in the cubicle to let the sedatives wear off. She told me that the procedure had lasted about an hour and that I had been back in the cubicle for nearly an hour, sleeping off the medication. I was amazed; I had little memory of ever leaving the cubicle. Two hours had passed. I thought that I was still waiting to go. Then vaguely I remembered the ride down the hall and the conversations with the doctors. But that was only minutes ago, I felt. The last thing I did remember was asking the doctor how much sedative he was going to give me; it was all coming back to me. I didn't feel drowsy or as if I had even had any medication. It was as though I had simply fallen asleep and was just waking up, ready to go home. The chocolate nurse came in and asked me how I felt. When I told her that I felt fine, she suggested that I take my time and relax for a little longer. She assured me that I would certainly feel the medication if I tried to get up and walk right away. So, I lay there, questioning Joan about the time, wondering if she were sure that much time had elapsed. She quieted me when she pointed to the clock on the opposite side of the room. It was eleven forty-five. I had been gone and unconscious for about two hours.

Suddenly I felt a pressure in my abdomen and my initial reaction was alarm. I pressed my abdomen slightly just as the nurse parted the curtain and entered the cubicle again. At that very same instant I heard a long, high-pitched sound that I could only describe as a long, loud whine. It must have lasted twenty seconds. Joan looked at me; I looked at her and the nurse said, "Yes, that's good; you'll get rid of all that gas." I had just made the longest, loudest, perfect-pitched super fart of my life. I was impressed. What impressed me was the fact that I wasn't even trying, and I could still fart like a bull. The doctor did say that the procedure would call for air to be injected into my intestinal tract, but I didn't think they meant enough to float a boat. After another loud but shorter outburst, I thought I was out of air because the pressure in my abdomen was no longer there. I was wrong. I pushed very slightly and again there was a long, loud one that came from under my hospital gown. Suddenly the ass-out hospital gown seemed like the most practical thing in the world; it was obviously meant for moments like this.

I thought about the late sixties when I lived in West Africa as a Peace Corps Volunteer. During the holidays, all the volunteers met in some predetermined city and partied for the duration of the holiday break. Instead of turkey and dressing for dinner, the daily fair was 'rice-chop', a heaping pile of rice covered with either groundnut stew or a cassava and fish stew. Either way, the results were the same, big-time gas. And after drinking enough beer to float the Titanic, the guys who were still capable would hold a little contest. The object of the contest was to see who could burst a balloon-with a fart. The only catch was that the fart had to be lit with a match. After more long swigs on the beer, down came the pants and out came assess. The secret was to keep your shorts up. The novice wouldn't know that. We saw some nasty ass burns from those who didn't know, and the rule was that you were not supposed to tell the newcomers the secret. They were always invited to go first. The key to success was timing. The experts would hold their breaths, if possible, push and light the match at just the right instant. It's hard to imagine a foot-long, blue flame shooting out of a human ass. The winner was always the one who destroyed the balloon. Reflecting, the sport seemed primitive compared to what I had done in the hospital recovery room.

There was no smell; I was clean inside. Suddenly Joan said, "Shhh! Listen!". I held my breath for a second to listen for whatever it was she was hearing. From across the corridor came another high-pitched, ten second fart that was a perfect counterpoint to mine. I laughed. Then unbelievably, from down the corridor came another, and yet another. There must have been four other patients in the cubicles who had just undergone the same procedure that I had. I thought of the scene from the movie, "Close Encounters of the Third Kind", where the alien mother ship was attempting to communicate with the humans on the mountaintop that served as a landing site. All they used were five simple tones, one note at a time. Before they got it right, the aliens shattered a few windows and caused some eardrums to pop. But once they got the volume and the notes right, it was pure music. I mentally assigned numbers to each cubicle. Number one was across from me. I was number two. Three and four were a few feet further down the corridor. One. One/Three. Three/One/Two. Four/Two/One. Again: Four/Two/One. Once more. Harmony! Joan was blind with tears from laughing. I pushed again. We were the new University of Chicago Gastrointestinal Harmony Ensemble, and we were good. Even the nurse couldn't stop laughing.

Joan looked outside of the curtain just as a new male patient entered the corridor, escorted by a nurse, for the same procedure. As he walked by, the expression on his face said it all. Joan closed the curtain and broke into hysterics. She described the man as walking through the corridor looking like he was in the *Twilight Zone*, wondering what the hell was going on. He had no idea that he had entered a concert. After another half hour or so, I felt comfortable enough to start getting dressed. It had been one very interesting morning; it was still early, only twenty five after twelve. I got dressed and thanked the nurse for her assistance as Joan and I left the cubicle and left the corridor. As I put my jacket on, I heard number Three bid me a farewell. Then number One said goodbye. It was touching and I wanted to cherish the memories. I held my head high as we stepped up to the desk to check out. I could still hear the Ensemble faintly in the background. The nurse at the desk wished us a good day as we walked through the archway that led to the bank of elevators. I turned and looked back at the unit and as the elevator doors opened and I blew out my final good-bye.

Las Palmas Jingle Bells

My first Christmas away from home was in Las Palmas, Canary Islands, a Spanish possession, off the west coast of Africa, near Morocco. The islands experience tropical weather year-round and have beautiful beaches; it was the place for young folks to be if you were leaving Europe during the holidays. From the north, students swarmed out of Spain, France, and Germany and as far away as Italy to celebrate in the balmy air of the tropical islands. From the south we flooded out of West Africa: Sierra Leone, Liberia, Senegal, all heading north to the party spot in the Atlantic. Lou and I went together along with a dozen other Peace Corps volunteers from across West Africa. One of the first people Lou and I met was Didier Alann, the Frenchman. Didier was cool, international. He was the same age as we were but worldly. Didier was very handsome, and suave, a cross between Dean Martin and Prince. Everything about him exuded confidence, yet he was comical and warm. He was bumming just like the rest of us, looking for an enjoyable time. Back home in Paris his family had money but for the time being, Didier was doing his own thing. He became my most trusted friend while we partied and traveled around Europe together. He spoke French, Dutch and other languages. When we first met in Las Palmas, he felt like an old friend right from the beginning. He was impressed that we had come from America to live in the 'jungle'. I promised to visit him whenever I got to France.

Four of us rented two rooms at the Residencia Syria, Luis Mortre, 27 in Las Palmas. From there we moved to the Mar Azul on Paseo De Las Canteras, and closer to the action spots. Students from all over Europe and Africa converged on the tiny islands, if not Las Palmas, then Tenerife Island a few miles away. There were more girls than guys on the island at one time than I had ever even imagined. That meant that our "get lucky" favorability ratings skyrocketed. Chances of getting lucky shot through the roof. It was then that I saw the most beautiful woman I'd ever seen in my life. She was purple black with features that were cut from black marble. I stared. Her hair was black as night with a radiance that seemed mystical. Her eyes were piercing and deep blue. I was not the only one staring at her; she had captivated everybody she passed. Ethiopian, she was breathtakingly beautiful. It was hard for me to imagine a woman so beautiful that she literally leaves you speechless.

Sitting in an open café under a bright warm sun, I was relaxing alone, when a group of young women gathered near the entry way. There were dozens of girls, girls everywhere. Most were students. The guys were outnumbered at least four to one. A big crowd was forming near the entrance to the patio where I was sitting and over all the heads of the crowd, I could see Lou. He was right smack in the middle of all the hyperactivity, talking and joking with everybody, especially the young women. They thought he was so charming. He was charming. Lou, from Minnesota, was the proverbial tall, dark, and handsome brother that girls dream about. As I continued to watch, he headed in my direction. In tow were two beautiful girls, holding each by the hand, one from France, the other from Belgium. If I had tried to write down what happened next and sell it as an idea, nobody would buy it; they just wouldn't believe it. I wouldn't have believed it. Lou introduced me to Rita and her friend Anna. As we were being introduced, Rita who was from Antwerp, Belgium, moved closer to the table and sat on my side, next to me. I reached out to offer my hand for support if she needed it. It was just an instinctive motion. She took my hand as we both sat back down next to each other. Lou began the conversation with one of his quips that got us all laughing. Lou ordered a round of drinks. The conversation grew as we got more comfortable.

Half an hour later Rita was still holding my hand. Somehow, we had come to know each other without the normal small talk. Lou and Anna both noticed that Rita and I had become fixated on one another. My new mate, Rita Curvier had just left her family to attend university in France. She was twenty-one years old and studying European History in Paris where she became friends with Anna. They were dorm mates at school. When she wasn't at school, Anna lived in Paris with her older sister who was a third-year medical student. Anna was studying architecture. Both Anna and Rita came from upper middle-class backgrounds with well-educated parents. Of the four of us at the table at that moment, two of us had graduated college and gotten degrees and the other two were currently in college working toward degrees. Both young ladies were impressed at the fact that both Lou and I had graduated from college, left our country and chosen to go live in Africa. Somehow, we were super dudes. We seemed very mysterious and exciting to them. And the fact that we were both black added to our 'mystique'. This was the first time I had seen Lou so content. He and Anna were the perfect couple. She was teaching him the rudiments of French. He wasn't doing very well. That only led to more laughter as we ordered another round of drinks. I asked the girls why they would leave a crowd of hundreds of people from all parts of the world, in every color imaginable, and choose Lou, a black guy and follow him to meet another black guy. For a moment they pretended not to understand the question. But after a few moments of mumbling communications between themselves, they both broke into giggles then loud laughter. They never answered the question. Lou and I looked at each other and said: "Cool."

After that first day, the four of us were inseparable. There were parties every night of the week in Las Palmas with music a constant buzz in the air. Some parties were private, but the best ones were the ones where we arrived by 'accident' and nobody knew anybody initially. By the time the parties were in full swing, everybody knew everybody. Didier also made friends easily. Girls were attracted to him like he was a movie star. He shared his good fortune with us whenever he could, introducing us to his friends, most of whom were girls. Didier broke away from our hotel after the first night and stayed in another hotel with one of the young ladies that he met. Our romances lasted for one week until it was time for us all to head back to our respective worlds. Before we left the island, Rita wrote down her address and phone number in Antwerp and asked that I promise to keep it in my passport so I wouldn't lose it. I promised. On the plane back to Freetown, Lou and I discussed our good fortune. He promised Anna he was going to visit her in Paris as soon as his tour was over. There would be so much to write about when I got back upcountry to Bunumbu.

Jonathan Kim

Episode 2: Jihii

Every morning there was a line out the door of the Medici Café for those waiting to get morning coffee and a roll. Inside, lined up along the big windows stood four tall round tables with stools for those lucky enough to get to them. Each tabletop was over Jonathan's head, so he had to climb up on a stool if he had any hope of seeing all the activity around him. Students from around the world who attended the University of Chicago could be seen lining up to be served. The Medici was the most popular eating spot in the university campus area. And there were always lots of pretty college girls-even on Saturdays. Jonathan and I became regulars at the morning coffee line up at the Medici. It wasn't long before all the employees knew Jonathan and whenever he came into the shop, he went right to the front of the line, waving his money and completely ignoring the waiting customers. Nobody seemed to mind. Whenever possible we just grabbed one of the tall tables and staked it out. Jonathan always ordered a croissant and hot chocolate; I always had coffee. Then one morning I had a great idea. There were so many university girls coming into the café that I decided to get a few names and numbers. Jonathan was my partner and I had to admit, he was charming and adorable. Whenever I saw a young lady that I wanted to meet, I would have Jonathan playfully meander up to her and smile. He never failed to get a warm smile in response. He would often say something like: "Are you a student? What's your name? My name is Jonathan! I'm five years old", before anyone could respond. By then everybody who was a regular in the café knew Jonathan and never failed to engage him in conversation. Charles, the young man who worked behind the counter complained that Jonathan was getting more names and numbers than he was. The staff and Kirsten, the owner of the cafe, liked Jonathan so much that they often gave him his order for free. We were beginning to make a name for ourselves. At least Jonathan was making a name for himself.

One morning as I got Jonathan seated and began drinking my coffee, I noticed a very cute Asian girl sitting alone near the door. She was absorbed in her laptop as the customers lined up placing their orders. It was an especially busy morning; the place was crowded as people scrambled to get condiments and exit near the end of the line. As we sat, I stared at the young lady at the other table, and we made eye contact. She noticed the two of us together and she smiled. I decided to put Jonathan to work. Unless you spoke softly, everyone in the place could hear your conversation. There was a constant buzz of conversation going on. Having given Jonathan his cue, I casually looked out the window as he climbed down from his stool and walked over to the other table where the young lady was seated. She instantly looked down at him and gave him a big smile and a handshake. They exchanged a few words then Jonathan abruptly turned and headed back toward me, everybody smiling at him as he crunched past them. Halfway back to my table, Jonathan looked right at me and belted out: "Denver, she's got a funny name and I forgot it. You have to ask her for it yourself!" The entire café exploded in laughter. Every customer and employee was looking right at me, laughing like crazy. I was so busted. Sheepishly I returned the smiles as Jonathan climbed back up on his stool and continued to eat his croissant. From across the room, I could see the young woman wiping her eyes as she tried to control her laughter. Thanks, Jonathan!

When we finished our food, we had to walk by the young woman to exit the café, so I put on my brave face and directed Jonathan to the door. Just as I passed her, our eyes met, and I smiled; she couldn't help but burst into laughter again. She said softly as she spoke through her tears: "My name is Jihii." I had the perfect response, "Hi, Jihii. My name is Denver and I suppose you've already met my therapist." That comment sent her into another episode of uncontrollable laughter. "Did you know that in Buddhism, the word 'jihi' means mercy and compassion?" "No, I didn't know that. Thank you." she said as I turned to Jonathan and told him to say goodbye to Jihi. He looked at me, then back at her as we walked out, and then he said, "Goodbye! Jihii! Denver wanted your phone number 'cause he likes you. He said you were cute. But you got a funny name!"

Kim of Destiny

In 1958 I was a sophomore in high school. I still wondered what my purpose in life was when one little girl made it very clear to me that I had no purpose in life. I was sixteen years old, and she was three. We had a love/hate relationship. I loved her. She hated me. Her name was Kim. She was one of seven children. Her oldest brother, Michael, a high school basketball player, was about my age and one of my close friends. Kim had gray-green eyes and soft, shiny sandy, blonde hair that touched her shoulders with strands of it always in her mouth. Her complexion was like a light chocolate milk shake. She reminded me of a tiny mermaid. She was beautiful. My heart belonged to Kim. There was only one problem. Kim totally denied my existence. I tried bribery, flattery, promises, anything just to get her attention. She always kept her distance and just stared at me. Her entire family knew that she and I had this weird, non-relationship and they thought it was funny. I wondered how I had developed such a strange relationship with this beautiful little girl. Michael and I were good friends, and he knew how much I was enraptured by his little sister. Under no circumstances would she speak to me or acknowledge me in any way, except to stare. And she kept her distance even in the presence of her brothers and sisters, even when her parents were around. She flatly refused to allow me into her world, and I couldn't fathom why. I had never experienced anything like that before and I was baffled. When I spoke to her, she just kept her distance and continued to stare at me coldly. She had no reason to dislike me; I had always been nice to her. Candy that I offered had to go through one of her sisters before she would accept it. Nothing I did ever made a difference. Why my relationship with a little girl named Kim was so important to me was a mystery. And for whatever reason, it only made me think about my life even more. Why was Kim even in my life, I wondered. I wondered what there was about my life that repulsed a little girl whom I had known all her life. She had imbedded herself deep into my consciousness. I doubted that I would ever forget her. Often when I was able talk to her from many yards, I made her a promise that one day we'd meet again and be friends. She just stared at me with an amplified indifference. Kim never spoke a word to me.

EAST MEETS WEST

At about 5:20pm on Saturday, January 31, 1981, Chicago's Union Station was buzzing with activity. Over five hundred NSA men, women and children began boarding a brand-new Amtrak train bound for Dallas, Texas. This new train was eight cars long and NSA was taking up five of the eight cars. Each NSA car was a neighborhood; each set of seats was a household. The train was alive. The members in each car began chanting *Nam-myoho-renge-kyo* softly and continued for the next hour or so. Each car agreed to do gongyo at the same time so that there would be complete harmony on the train. After prayers, families and members ate their prepared meals and continued the lively chatter throughout the train. After dinner the conversations really began. There were celebrations and parties happening in every car. I could walk from one car to the next and it was like walking down the street, meeting friends and neighbors as I entered different blocks. The celebrations went on. The next day, February 1st, we pulled into the Dallas Reunion Station. I had no idea of the significance of the name Reunion Station until we were heading back to Chicago.

We were welcomed by the Young Men's Division Brass Band, members from the Dallas area and the Drum Corps of the Japanese members who had come from Japan to support this cause for kosen rufu (world peace). As we exited the train, the band played, and a line was formed on each side of us as everyone applauded and we happily marched and danced into the station. From the entrance of the station all along the corridors inside, leading to the main terminal, Japanese members were lined up to greet us and shake our hands. The big surprise came when we entered the big hall of the main terminal where, to our amazement, were more than a thousand members greeting us with a spirited version of their hometown song: *"Deep in the Heart of Texas"*. After a brief meeting with the General

Director, and other dignitaries, the members took recess for a few hours to have lunch and prepare for the *"East Meets West"* culture festival to be held later at the Reunion Arena, just across the street from the station.

The program opened with the dynamic Fuji Fife and Drum Corps. Their spirited play and unity had the entire audience on its feet giving full approval to the performance. The next part of the show surprised members as well as non-members because riding out on horseback in full samurai warrior costume, representing 'the East' was Toshiro Mifuni, the famous Japanese actor (Torinaga) of *Shogun* fame. Riding out onto the stage from the opposite direction in full cowboy attire, representing 'the West' was Patrick Duffy of '*Dallas*' fame. Both Mifuni and Duffy were practicing Nichiren Buddhists. The two riders met in the middle of the stage and shook hands. This brought an extended standing ovation from the audience. The program continued with one outstanding presentation after another. The festival was magnificent.

By the time all the festivities were over and everyone who had traveled from Chicago had boarded the train to return home; we were all exhausted. It felt good to sit down and relax as the train slowly left the station headed back to Illinois. The entire trip and festival had been a complete success. The ride back was more subdued than the ride down. Having expended so much energy shouting and screaming at the festival, most of the members just laid back and engaged in low key conversations as they enjoyed the soothing sounds of the train rolling along the tracks. I felt rejuvenated as I strolled down the aisle of one car and into the next, greeting members as I went along. All along the aisles you could hear lively conversations about the festival.

And then as I continued my stroll, I heard someone in a conversation say "Gary". I immediately shouted, "I'm from Gary!" When I located the section of the car that the comment had come from, I approached it and repeated, "Hey, I'm from Gary!" There was a group of young women engaged in a very lively conversation, laughing, and having a wonderful time. Mixed among them were three small children, two of them playing amongst themselves. But the third, a beautiful little girl of about three years old, stood there on the seat just staring at me. Our eyes locked as soon as I walked up. Her stare intensified as I introduced myself to the group of young women. Strangely I felt I knew this little girl but that was impossible. Everything about her seemed familiar, her sandy brown hair, her gray-green eyes and most of all, her attitude, her cold stare. Stranger yet, she looked at me like she recognized me. We both stood there, eyes locked on each other when a female voice said, "I'm from Gary and you do look familiar". I introduced myself to the group and let them know that I was born and raised in the 'Steel City' and that she looked familiar to me, too. In quick response, the young lady asked, "Do you know any Morrises?" Braggingly, I replied, "Yeah, I know some Morrises: I know a Michael, a Craig, a Crosby, a Shane, a Kim, and a Denise. They lived down the street from me, across from the Stewart House on 15th & Massachusetts Street. Our eyes met and locked as I shouted, "You're Denise Morris, aren't you?" At that moment I could tell she recognized me because she paused for a moment, stood up as she approached me and gave me an enormous smile and said, "No, Denise is my older sister. I'm Kim!" I screamed, "KIM!" It was my little Kim from 15th and Massachusetts St whom I had not seen since she was three years old. We gave each other a huge bear hug. I had Kim laughing to tears when I told her how she used to treat me when she was three years old. Never a word would she utter to me; she would just stare at me, exactly the way the little girl standing on the seat was staring at me now. Kim was now twenty-five years old with a daughter of her own and her daughter was the little girl who was standing on the seat staring at me. And the little girl's name was-Kim. It was deja-vu all over again. We both laughed until it hurt. Kim had excused herself from her friends and we sat together and talked for hours as the train rolled on toward Chicago. Kim had begun practicing Nichiren Buddhism only a year or so earlier and this was her first trip with the organization. She gave me her address and phone number and we promised to stay in touch. The reunion took me back deep into my memories and how she had affected me when she was a baby and how I had promised her that we would meet again and become friends. I had kept my promise. My life surely had a purpose. Her daughter, Kim, Jr., who was three years old, had other ideas as she stared at me the whole time; she never spoke a word to me.

Guess What

Thoughts of a Substitute Teacher.

I was substitute teacher working at a west-side district charter school in Washington, D.C. I had extensive teaching experience, having taught in Africa, and at various levels from pre-school through college in U.S. I was at my very best when sharing ideas and challenging young, curious minds. The students appreciated the personal attention that I extended to anyone of them needing extra assistance. Though I was small in stature, I enjoyed the respect that the students showed me. Most of my students, both male and female towered over me. The girls took delight in knowing that I felt no unease when they joked with me about my height. I'd say to the boys, "You're just tall-that's all" and the girls loved it. I enjoyed the levity as much as they did. At every school location I swore that I had seen it all. But every new assignment proved me wrong. I understood that the way to reach someone's heart, especially young people, was to open mine. One on one life experiences were especially rewarding. From early in my life, I had been driven by a passion for teaching and opening young minds with great ideas. It was important to me that my students became critical thinkers. Flashbacks from my childhood convinced me that asking questions and taking action was the route to understanding; and for me, understanding was far more important than just knowing. This was the message I intended to leave with my students

Eastern High School in Washington, D.C. was the same high I had taught at when I was training for Peace Corps. Ron Jackson, my Peace Corps Volunteer colleague from Philadelphia and I had walked the same halls decades earlier. Froebel High School in Gary came back to mind. When I was a student at Froebel, students were on parade as they strolled down the long halls, laughing, dancing and performing whatever act they could to draw attention to themselves. The boys were always trying to draw the attention of the girls who lined both sides of the hall. High school was exciting. As a senior I enjoyed feeling the energy of all my schoolmates as they scurried here and there on their way to classes. Fitted button up sweaters and long skirts were the 'uniform' of the day for the girls. They wore penny loafers, often with a shiny new dime inserted in the little slot atop the shoe. A single strand of fake pearls usually completed their outfits. There could be no loud music playing in the halls. Boys laughed and flirted; girls giggled and pretended to ignore them. All was innocent and not at all removed from an atmosphere of warmth, camaraderie. High school was the time of growth, experimentation and looking toward the future. Students averaged sixteen years of age; some looked much older than their years. However, the teachers at Froebel High and my earlier grammar school were not to be ignored or disrespected. Teachers had the last word. There was no arguing with the teacher; what they said was the law-period. Any students dumb enough or stupid enough to argue with a teacher, let alone hit a teacher was destined for defeat if not destruction. Any offense at school was usually relayed home before the student got home. It was not unusual to get punished at school and then get punished again once you got home. Teachers held a position of respect and admiration. Parents looked to the teachers as leaders in the community who dedicated their lives to serving the youth so any youngster who violated that honor was heading for serious trouble. Absences, unless verified and authorized by the parent, were rare. I went through all of grammar school without missing one day of school. It was a good thing, too, because the city had truant officers who rode around the city daily. If they came across kids who were not in school, they would pick them up and take them either home or to school, often warning the parents not to let the child get picked up again. Students and parents alike held teachers in very high esteem. If you didn't like what the teacher said, too bad. Earlier, in grade school, boys even got paddled if they were caught fighting. They would have to report to the coach and told to bend over and take a few whacks to the butt with a wooden paddle that had holes drilled into it. Few boys fought in school again after that ordeal. In a way the relationship between teachers, students and parents was sacred. But when I was a kid, it was hard for me to imagine a teacher having a life outside of the classroom. Teachers didn't eat; they didn't sleep or go shopping or have sex. It seemed they were above the common fray of everyday life that we students and other ordinary people endured. Outside of class, teachers did not exist.

At Eastern High School testosterone fueled the male students, especially the athletes. I was perfectly comfortable, acknowledging the different students as they reached out to give me a fist bump and say good morning as they entered my classroom. Every classroom had its own "celebrity" student. One was a tall, lanky sixteen year older. He was six feet two and an NBA wannabe; and for that I called him "MJ". He relished the idea of being identified with such an icon even though he knew full well that I was making fun of him. He called me Mr. Short. MJ was a smart, funny student and I liked him a lot. Though he was often silly beyond his years, he was always mannerly, even in his antics. He was talented and intelligent, but he preferred comedic antics instead of being serious about his schoolwork. We had bonded almost immediately when we first met. It would have been hard for me not to find him likeable. Oftentimes the class and I would all sit and share his antics as he dominated the room. MJ was not a bad kid or even a problem kid. He just liked to show off from time to time. I understood that. But there was a time and a place to show off and it was my job, my responsibility to let him know that my classroom was neither.

During one of his episodes, I walked up to him and as he drew cartoons and nonsense on the board, I reached under his long arms and erased it all. The class laughed and applauded. He glared down at me. I glared back up at him. We stared each other down for what seemed like forever. I never blinked; he blinked, and he knew he had lost that challenge. The class roared with laughter. At that moment, it was clear who had the moral and mental strength to prevail. I asked him why he took it upon himself to clutter the board with nonsense. It was the second time that he had come into the room and cluttered the board with his nonsensical scribblings and drawings. His classroom behavior was no better than his study habits. Then I had a great idea!

The following day was much a repeat of the previous day except that when the class was dismissed and the students dispersed, I went down to the gym where all the guys spent most of their spare time. It was also where my favorite class clown was doing his gymnastic performance on the basketball court. Soon the group of players had chosen up teams and began a full court game with MJ leading the way as only he could. He was looking very efficient at his game and drawing the attention and admiration from the onlookers. When he saw me watching him, he really began to put on a show. I was impressed. Then I put my plan into action. During a break, I walked right into the huddle and stood near MJ who had the ball. The weirdest look came over his face as he stared down at me standing next to him waiting for the game to continue. Once the game started again, I followed my guy all over the court, everywhere. I didn't try to block his shots, I just followed him as best I could. I followed him up the court, down the court I was behind him all over the court. After a few minutes I had to stop, bend over, put my hands on my knees and take a deep breath. The game continued around me. Once I caught my breath, I was back in the game, following MJ's every step. The crowd had grown larger, and I could hear the loud cheers, "Mr. Long! Mr. Long! Mr. Long!" Before long there were a few teachers watching the game, cheering me on. My students who were in my class realized what was happening and explained it to the other teachers. MJ's game deteriorated right before our eyes; he missed shots, lost the ball to the opposition, and stumbled badly as he tried to recover from his flub. As more and more students started watching and screaming, my star player finally stopped and shouted out as everybody, including myself, burst into laughter. I was still on the court, exhausted but determined to stay out there if the game went on. The game finally ended. MJ's team lost. He just stared at me as the crowd grew and the laugher got louder and louder. I slowly walked off the court to applause and into the crowd, getting pats on the back as I struggled to catch my breath. I had won. From then on, when MJ attended my classes, guess what!

Curse of the Bundus and Poros

Back in Gary, Fred used to say, "It in but not of it." By now I was well established in the village and on campus. I was 'in it'. I learned that I wasn't 'of it' when a curse was put on me by the villagers. It was serious to the villagers but not to me-at first. In my mind it had just been one big misunderstanding. In Sierra Leone, West Africa, around September or October the surrounding villages initiate the boys and the girls into their respective secret societies. It's a coming-of-age ritual. For the girls it's the Bundu society and for the boys, it's the Poro society. I learned that akin to freemasonry, the Poro is an organization, made up of tribesmen who hold power within the tribes, its highest-ranking member being called Kashi in Temne and Taso in Mende. I had met the leader in the village when I went with Sam to the market to buy bush beef. The Poro is responsible for carrying out the annual initiations for the boys. The entire initiation process is very secretive. Everyone in the region knows that during the night ceremonies, especially during the night march, foreigners should shutter their windows and not come outside or look outside until the end of the night's ceremonies.

But I had already scheduled a date with the young lady next door, a beneficial friend. She was only a few dozen yards down the footpath, and I knew the path blindfolded. I had showered and sprayed on some men's cologne that Sam had bought at George the Lebanese's roadside store. It smelled like a blend of bacon, perfume, and ammonia. Anyone could smell me coming yards away. But after a few minutes and with some fresh air my nose got used to it or became so numb that I couldn't smell myself. I turned down the kerosene lamp and I cracked one of the shutters just wide enough peek out. As far as I could see into the total dark distances were torches for miles, winding their way to the ceremonial grounds in the far distance. It was a sight to behold. The distant sound of drums filled the night air. It was a magical experience. I closed the shutter, slipped to the side door and tip toed across the yard into the bush and onto the footpath. All I could think about was helping my neighbor test her new mosquito netting until morning. I knew every step of the way to her door. Follow the footpaths. Snakes hate footpaths. It was pitch black. Quietly I counted the steps to her door and just as I counted to the halfway point, somebody touched me.

I immediately heard what I recognized as a mixture of pissed-off Krio, Mende and Temne coming from all around me. Someone was holding onto my arm, then the other. I wondered why anybody (other than me) would be walking around in the dark during secret society ceremonies. It could have been my cologne, but I knew I blew it when I opened my mouth and said, "Hey, what the #@!^$%!" That gave me away for sure. Shortly several voices had surrounded me in the dark when someone lit a torch, revealing all our faces in the bright orange flickering light. "MEESTAH LONG!!!!", someone shouted. There was quite a commotion as more bodies gathered around me, bringing more and more torches to the area. In only a couple of minutes it became quite a scene. My mind was racing. Before long it was a major scene. Then I recognized one of the men. My dear friend Adbul Kanu was taking part in the ceremony and was one of the bodies surrounding me. He discreetly directed me to turn around and quietly go back into my house and he would talk to me later. As I turned timidly and began to tiptoe away, I asked nervously, "Hey, Abdul these brothers ain't gonna' kill me for trying to get some pussy, are they?"

When I saw Abdul a few days later, he was angry with me as he informed me that the village had collectively put a curse on me. I felt relieved. I had expected the penalty to be more severe. Besides, I didn't believe in curses anyway. They're superstition. I thought even "Reb" back home at the Stewart Settlement House would agree with me on that. I didn't worry or even think about it anymore until the night chanting started. Every night at around sunset women from the village gathered at the foot of my incline and began a mournful, sorrowful, moaning chant that went on all night. It was a chant for the dead. Some left, others came. Children stopped talking to me when they saw me. They ran away, knowing that I was a dead man. People up and down the road that usually spoke and passed the time with small talk, ignored me. "Bua!", I'd say. I got nothing back. Scariest of all was when none of my students came to classes. I was avoided like the plague. Sometimes stray chickens would cross our property. Sam said that they were fair game so from time to time, we had unexpected chicken dinner. Even the chickens stopped crossing our yard. It went on for a week. I asked Abdul how long the curse was supposed to last. He laughed as usual and said that the villagers were surprised that I was still alive. Abdul laughed, obviously knowing more than I did. When I thought about the incident later, I understood how the curse could affect people in a frighteningly negative way. Perhaps had I been born in Sierra Leone, I would have acted in a different way. As an American, my perspective seemed to have affected the outcome. Admittedly, my nerves were beginning to fray after the first week. The one who is cursed begins to experience a sense of total isolation. In my case it went from isolation to paranoia. But my instincts kept telling me to stick with reason. Despite my own beliefs, I was getting really scared for a while. I thought about the Mau Mau uprising in Kenya earlier in the century and how the natives invaded British homes in the night and massacred families in their beds. The victims never knew who their assailants were. It could have been their cook or their gardener or the driver. I thought about Sam and Lammi. It would have been just like Sam to hide under my bed, waiting for me. Then my sleep began to suffer; my appetite disappeared. At that point I had to slap myself back to reality. The power of the curse was that the people believed it based on what their environment suggested. Intuitively I felt just the opposite. The effects of my environment, though frightful, were determined by my state of mind, nothing else. I gave myself another mental slap and all was well. What I had to do was find the positive in the situation. It was not hard to do. Eventually everything returned to normal, and my prurient interests were held in check during the next initiation season. The history of the village of Bunumbu would thereafter show that in the year of nineteen hundred and sixty-eight, a powerful Mende man from America, came to Bunumbu and repelled a Poro and Bundu curse. This great Mende man would come to be known as Meestahlongbangbang.

Jonathan Kim

Episode 3: Ray School Playground

Jonathan and I became regulars at the Medici Cafe. Everybody knew him and looked forward to his little antics. We were the *'Odd Couple' of 57ᵗʰ Street*. People I had been seeing regularly began speaking to me with smiles whenever they saw us together. Those same strangers would also ask about him if ever they saw me alone. On one of our excursions, a woman who had seen us together many times asked how long I had been babysitting Jonathan. I laughed and told her to ask Jonathan how long I had been his babysitter. When he heard the question, he looked up at the woman, indignant, with a furrowed brow and said, "Denver is not my babysitter. I am not a baby, and I don't need a babysitter. Denver is my friend." Then he strolled off. I reiterated the same sentiments to the woman who seemed taken aback by Jonathan's blunt, intelligent response. It was true. Though Jonathan and I spent hours together every Saturday, neither he, his mother nor I ever considered me his babysitter. The fact was: Jonathan was my dear little friend and I loved hanging out with him. He just happened to be four years old and better company than most adults. We explored every business along the avenue, from the bookstore on one end to the noodle shop on the other.

One of Jonathan's favorite spots was the playground across the street at the Ray Elementary School. We would spend hours wrestling in the grass and running after each other. We always got passersby's' attention when we played karate masters. Jonathan would scream at me and charge. I would scream back, charge and slam him gently to the ground, appearing to have really hurt him. He loved it. Then I would let him jump up and down on me pretending to stomp me into submission. Oftentimes when we looked up, there would be people looking at us, puzzled as we attacked one another, screaming at the top of our lungs, and throwing ferocious karate chops. I loved every minute of it as much as Jonathan did. Sometimes Jonathan would go straight to the sand box and get so absorbed in his play that he would forget I was there. Sometimes he would race to the swings and demand that I push him higher than any of the other kids in the swings.

I remember one trip to the park that I still laugh about today. It was a very warm summer day and the children's waterspout was on. It was a tall pole that stood about twelve feet high with a circular spout at the top that forced water out in a big circular spray area where the children could stand in the downpour. Children in tiny bathing suits screamed with delight as they ran back and forth through the water, soaking themselves from head to toe. Jonathan stood there, fully clothed, looking at me then looking at the waterspout. I could see in his eyes what he was thinking, and I shouted out to him across the distance, "Don't even think about it!" Parents who were sitting nearby around the spout watching their children noticed the drama unfolding with Jonathan and me. They had seen us in the park before, so they knew who we were. Again, I warned Jonathan: "Jonathan!". Then calmly and deliberately Jonathan walked right into the circular downpour of water, fully dressed. He stood there under the waterfall, arms crossed, looking at me, laughing like a maniac. The parents sitting nearby and the other children playing in the water broke into hysterics, staring at Jonathan as he just stood there under the waterfall, looking at me, laughing. I was shocked but fully amused at his stunt. People walking through the park noticed the prank and before long, Jonathan had an audience of laughing spectators. I had to laugh, too. It was a funny sight. We both laughed as we headed back to the cleaners, him leaving a trail of water with every step. Parents and children coming into the park took second glances at Jonathan as he passed them laughing hysterically, shaking off water as we left the playground. I said, "Jonathan, boy, your mother is going to kill you!" He laughed hysterically, looked me in the eye and said, "No, she's going to kill you!" *Touché,* Jonathan.

To the Principles' Office

The fundamental law of Nichiren Buddhism is Nam-myoho-renge-kyo and the Law protects those who propagate and practice accordingly. From the first day of my classes at Westwood College, I strongly encouraged all my students to ask questions. In fact, I used the phrase, "Ask questions until you understand." That did not necessarily mean asking me, but to continue asking questions until the answers were found. Students were delighted with that notion and often wondered aloud how I could know so much. So, during one of my humanities classes, the subject of religion came up with questions to me about my religious beliefs. I told the class that I was a Nichiren Buddhist. Then I briefly explained what the practice was about. Most of the students in the class were fascinated, having never known a 'Black Buddhist'. Like most, their idea of a Buddhist was of a bald, potbellied guy sitting in a lotus position. I clarified most of their misunderstandings. In that humanities class, we discussed disciplines like art, music, religion, dance, architecture, etc. A vibrant discussion ensued with most of the class taking part. But there were a couple of dissenters, protesting that the class and I were denigrating their religion by questioning and dissecting certain aspects of religion. I often reminded students that a critical thinker was one who always asked questions about any given topic when studying that topic. The annoyed students went to the newly appointed Director of Student Affairs with a complaint about me and the class talking about Christianity and Buddhism. They were also upset that most of the class was actively participating and asking quite relevant questions about both religions. Not long after, I received a notice to come to the director's office to discuss the matter. When the two or three disenchanted students heard that I had been called to the office, they were gleeful about my apparent plight, telling others that I was going to lose my job or at least get reprimanded and even be forced to apologize to them.

I arrived at the director's office, was invited in and offered a seat. As I sat down, she turned away from me, closed her office door, and turned around to look me right in the face and together we both exploded into laughter. The director was a new Women's Division SGI member who had just started practicing Buddhism a year or so earlier. She knew that I had been practicing for years. In fact, during the term before she became a director, she had sometimes sought me out to ask me questions about the practice. Our meeting ended in laughter, but I had to walk out with a straight face to avoid any suspicions. The complaining students never knew. From that day forward, no student ever complained about any of the discussions again. That was due in part to the fact that an excerpt of my graduate thesis from DePaul University, the story of how I met my wife, Joan, had been published in a book entitled, *The Buddha Next Door*, the sequel to *The Buddha in Your Mirror*, by Middleway Press. When I received my copy of the book, I immediately showed it to my Program Director, Mrs. Boston, whom I had grown to like very much, and she was pleased to have a new instructor come in with some published work to his credit. So, what does she do? At the faculty meeting, she holds the book up and starts talking about how "Denver has brought a new standard of professionalism and excellence to the faculty, yadda, yadda, yadda" and "We, the faculty should work harder to get published, etc. Please take a minute and stop by Denver's classes to congratulate him." By now every faculty member in the room was glaring at me with tight smiles and courteous nods of their heads. I wondered what Nichiren Daishonin would have done in a similar situation.

Sometimes during my classes, I wrote phrases on the board like: "Questions are the answer" or "Learn everything about everything" or "A sword in the hands of a coward is useless," hoping to spark critical thinking efforts in the class. Initially the students thought I was weird for asking the class to explain what they thought such phrases meant. In the context of the subject of humanities, anything could be discussed. My intention was to have the class get deeply involved in conversation about things they never thought about, have them start to ask questions about anything, everything. No subject was 'off-limit'. I had discovered that even when the opportunity availed itself, most of the students were reluctant to get 'invested'.

In one writing class a young lady said aloud, "Mr. Long, you make us do all this writing and reading of our stuff out loud. It's embarrassing!" She continued smugly: "Why don't you read some of your stuff out loud?" The entire class broke into laughter. I said, "Ok, Ms. Taylor, I will do just that and since you brought it up, you can come up front and read it for us, out loud!" I handed her my copy of *The Buddha Next Door*. The room fell silent as she began to read. Then she read the part about chanting Nam-myoho-renge-kyo. And just as she read the last few words, a deep male voice in the back of the room shouted out: "Yo, Dr. Long, what is Nam-myoho-renge-kyo?" "Yesss!" I thought. Later that evening I heard the highest compliment paid to me by one of my students. I was walking down the hall, passing a group of my female students going in the opposite direction when we all spoke: "Hello, Ladies", I said. "Hello, Professor Long", they all responded, giggling. Then it happened. One of the young ladies looking back at me and laughing aloud as they moved farther down the hall, shouted out: "Professor Buddha"!

I Apologize to Butterflies

When I look back over my life and realize the joy that it has brought, my appreciation for life abounds. I sit on the deck in my back yard cherishing wonderful memories and becoming one with the environment. We who are fortunate enough will one day be only memories. Those less fortunate will not. Memories are what make our lives worth having been lived. I remember reading: "The older I get, the earlier it gets late." Most of my life's memories are happy, fun-filled years. There were tough times too, but it seems to me that we hold on to those memories that either propel us forward or hold us back. I always chose to move forward. Even as a child, I surmised that this thing called "life" was really something special. It was much more than just my curious nature. I wondered why I have a curious nature; there must be some reason for it. My spiritual awareness caught me by surprise. I began to understand that my questions were being answered in the form of life experiences. It took a while, but I eventually got it. I'm still getting it. It is so easy to take life for granted. Soon enough we learn that the longer we live the more we realize how short life is. Such is the mind and realm of youth. I was young in years once, exploding with enthusiasm, ambition, and most of all curiosity. I wanted to know everything. I strove to accomplish that goal. But I understood nothing of patience, wisdom, and one's life's mission.

One day as I sat on the deck, I saw a swallowtail butterfly. It was a rare sight and I felt fortunate for having seen it. I immediately named it Flutter. It was beautiful; it flitted and flirted up down and around the yard. The sight of it took me back to up-country Sierra Leone, West Africa where I lived and taught for two years. The butterflies there were as big as your hands. There were swallowtails so big and beautiful that they took your breath away. Before I go into detailing my relationship with butterflies, I'm going to start from near the beginning.

When I first arrived in Africa, I was anxious about having a hobby, something to keep me busy, to keep my mind occupied so that I would not get bored. How little did I know. As I got settled in and began communicating with friends and family back home, my aunt granted one of my earlier wishes and sent me a nice archery set. As a kid, I loved archery. At one point my favorited possession was my lemonwood bow with blunted practice arrows. I loved that bow. But one day as I was stringing it, I broke it! I cried! My sister laughed! I beat her with it! She cried! Ok, so I received the archery set from my aunt and I quickly set up a functional target with my twelve-year-old helper, Sam's assistance. My target was set in front of the house across the width of the house and surrounded by heavy bush. Together Sam and I made sure that the target was thick enough and high enough so that I wouldn't lose my arrows if I missed, or if my arrow hit the target and went through it. We worked to keep the target far enough from the bush so that if I missed the target entirely, I'd still see my arrows. The hour finally came for me to test my skills and to bet Sam that I could outshoot him. He was chomping at the bit for the wager. We argued for few minutes about who was going first. It was my archery set. I was going first. I stood my ground, took my position, and fired the arrow. It hit the target but to the upper right. I shouted how good that was. Sam sneered. I shot again, the arrow went straight through dead center of the target and out through the back into the bush. Sam and I both just stood there and stared at each other not believing what we had just witnessed. Sam regained his composure first and headed to the target and the bush to find the arrow. As I reached the target, Sam shouted out, "Meestah Long, that shot was dead center. You hit two targets in one!" As I entered the underbrush and approached Sam, he pointed to my arrow which was stuck dead center of a small chimpanzee. I gave up archery.

Back to Flutter in my back yard. I thought deeply about the magnificent butterflies that I had seen and taken for granted every day in Bunumbu. Then I apologized to Flutter because one hobby I developed in the bush was butterfly collecting. Like before, my aunt back home had sent me a butterfly collection kit and I was excited-at first. I even began studying butterflies, especially swallowtails. To my surprise, I learned that the swallowtail, from the family Papilionidae has about 550 species. Papilio is Latin for butterfly. Most of the species are tropical and living on every continent except Antarctica. Every day I saw the most incredible butterflies that fluttered here, there, and everywhere I looked. On my way to the art building, I often stopped along the way to watch a butterfly do its thing. The most common swallowtail was the Tiger, named so because of its black and yellow striping. It was easy to spot, and it became so familiar to me that I began to ignore it with hopes of finding some of the more exotic varieties. Regardless of the genus of the butterfly, they were all gorgeous in their designs and coloration. I was so awe struck by the overwhelming symmetry of each insect. Word got out around campus that I was collecting butterflies and the students began bringing me butterflies that they had caught, most of which were in no shape to display. There were so many brought to me, not understanding the delicacy involved in catching them that I had to dissuade the students from continuing with their efforts. As I read increasingly about collecting, I had to learn how to catch them; they were so very delicate. The kit that my aunt sent me included instructions on how to catch a butterfly without damaging its wings. The big challenge was to catch a butterfly and disable it quickly without damaging it. The proper technique was quick and very effective. The proper way to get a good specimen was to catch it in mid aid with one quick swoop of the net. With a twist of the wrist, the netting would immobilize the butterfly. With one drop of the liquid provided in the kit on the thorax of the butterfly, it was dead. Then the specimen could be mounted. After a year, I had built quite an impressive collection. I was proud of my work and how much I had learned about butterflies and nature in the bush.

But that was many years ago and now as I sat on my deck in my back yard watching Flutter fly around freely in and out of the blossoms, my regret was palpable. Over the many years since my butterfly collecting days, I had come to learn and appreciate the respect and dignity owed to every living thing, especially butterflies. It was said that if you love a flower, you don't cut it; you let it live.

Butterflies were no different. With painful realization I accepted the fact that I had killed butterflies simply because they were beautiful. I apologize to butterflies.

Arshile Gorky

I did not want to go the art exhibit on North Michigan Ave. My design project at school had a long way to go before it was done, but attending the exhibit counted big time on my final grade, so I decided to go. It didn't occur to me at the time that just because I was a first-year student studying industrial design did not mean that I could ignore Modern Art or Art History courses, the latter of which I hated. It was Friday and nearing the Thanksgiving holiday. My original plan was to skip out right after class, go down to Randolph Street and catch the early South Shore train home to Gary. But having to attend the gallery exhibit meant that I would have to go several blocks north, past Randolph Street, up to 109 E. Ontario. Replacing that last class with a gallery exhibit did not appeal to me at all. My design professor required that every student in class would have to attend the exhibit, no exceptions! The show would only be there from November 8th to December 14th and today was already November 22nd. There might even be a quiz on the exhibit after the Thanksgiving break.

A bunch of us students decided to make the short hike north a fun event. As we lined up in front of the school, we all held hands, forming a line ten persons wide. It all began as we walked hand in hand down wide Michigan Avenue greeting the tourists and others who were strolling through Grant Park. Suddenly we were skipping together and laughing at how absurd the whole idea was. Surprisingly on-comers and other pedestrians laughed and smiled as we skipped past. Many pedestrians even stooped over and went under our outstretched arms, laughing along with the rest of us. The public was taking part and helping us create performance art. It was crazy and it was great fun. Even the police seemed to be enjoying our antics. The more people we encountered as we went forward, the funnier and more attention-grabbing it all became. By the time we reached Randolph St. the whole thing had become a spectacle. Somehow, we had even gotten the attention of people on the other side of Michigan Avenue. Downtown Chicago was being very receptive to a bunch of 'weirdo' Art Institute students. And a bunch of weirdos we were. I thought we looked like a wild punk-rock band. We were tall, short, male, female, straight, gay, Asian, Black, White. The word circus was a fitting description. If the group all came from that institution, the Art Institute of Chicago then it would be safe to assume that there was talent somewhere in the group. On cue Kay signaled for the group to turn and squat! The applause was even more surprising. Kay then directed everybody to "kick" and right legs, then left legs went up in an outrageous attempt to do the high kick of Broadway showgirls. In unison we all complied, and the optics were hilarious. Not everybody was able to kick up high and maintain balance. I think more people watching really wanted to join in since we were having so much fun. Our mood was even reflected in the weather. It was in the upper fifties in mid-November. And the sun was shining brightly. It was a beautiful day, and I was with my friends from school and Kay, my future girlfriend. Despite the fun I was having on the outside, inside I felt a lingering, haunting sense of gloom and foreboding. I could not explain it, but it was there; it was a darkness that had been with me most of the day even before we took off for the art gallery. I tried to ignore it, but it persisted.

Once we reached Randolph St., all the nonsense stopped. Traffic got heavy, and there were many more pedestrians. It was time to focus on where we were going. North Michigan Avenue was hustling and bustling. Busy people darted here, ran there as we crossed Michigan Ave to the west side of the street. Everybody was in a hurry. It was like watching a movie that was sped up, a giant ant colony in macrocosm. On closer inspection though I could see that people weren't talking to each other. Each person was in a hurry and other people seemed to just get in the way. I felt extremely fortunate to be in the group because we were serious students. I was also lucky to have a friend like Kay who was always with me when our schedules permitted. She had instigated much of silliness that sparked the gang into comic action.

We finally arrived at The Arts Club of Chicago 109 E. Ontario. Featured until December 4th was the *"Arshile Gorky Drawings"* exhibit. There was much I had yet to learn about Gorky. The first time I heard his name was when the class was instructed to come to his exhibit, and I had no idea what to expect from his art. Realizing that, I figured the worst that could happen was that I learn something new. The exhibit gallery seemed dark compared to the bright sunshine outside, but after a few minutes the lighting was perfect as my eyes adjusted to the quieter, softer light. For whatever reason, my inexplicable sense of gloom persisted as I read about the artist: "Arshile Gorky (Vosdanik Adoian) was born in Turkey on April 15, 1904, and he died on July 21, 1948, in Sherman, Connecticut. He had a short life of only forty-four years. That was a 'downer'.

His work was "a link between European Surrealists and American Abstract Expressionism", his bio read. I did not know that, so I had learned something new already. I continued reading about the artist's early life in Turkey where, when he was a kid, his father deserted the family to avoid the Turkish draft. In 1920 Gorky came to the United States to live with his sister in Watertown, Massachusetts. Once in America he assumed the name Arshile from *Achilles,* the brooding hero of the *Iliad.* His life was getting more interesting as I read on. In 1946 he lost many of his numerous paintings in a studio fire. Then he underwent surgery for cancer. The more I read about Gorky, the more depressed I got. I read what should have been enough about Arshile Gorky but I continued reading. In 1948 he broke his neck in an automobile accident, losing the use of his painting hand. What a downer, I thought. Then his wife left him. Finally, in the grand finale, Gorky hanged himself. His life story left me dreary and depressed. His biography was more compelling and dramatic than his paintings. What a downer.

As I continued viewing the drawings, I began to experience a very high-pitched ringing in my ears. At first, I thought it was just me, so I tried to ignore it. But it continued, increasing in intensity until it could no longer be ignored. Others in the gallery seemed to be experiencing the same phenomenon as people began to meander toward the door which led outside. I moved to the door and stepped outside into the bright light to escape the annoyance of the high-pitched ringing inside the gallery. As everyone exited the gallery, the ringing was real but no longer an issue. Instead something else was happening that was causing confusion and hysteria on the street. People were screaming, horns were blaring; others were running as if in madness. I could not tell what was going on but whatever it was, it was something big. Most of us walked over to Michigan Avenue and there was pandemonium. Police officers were running this way and that. Someone shouted out and asked one of the officers what was happening. His answer was short, blunt and brutal: "President John F. Kennedy's been shot in Dallas, Texas! He's dead! President John F. Kennedy is dead!" It took a moment for my mind to process what the officer had said and when it did, everything around me suddenly moved in slow motion. I could see people's mouths moving but no sounds were coming out. I could see men, women and children crying, tears flowing from faces, but there was no sound coming from them. My vision blurred from my tears as I slowly meandered down Michigan Avenue back toward Randolph Street. Groups of people gathered around a storefront where a television was broadcasting the latest news of the assassination.

Some guy named Lee Harvey Oswald had reportedly hidden out on the upper floor of a book depository and shot the president as his motorcade went by. There was mass hysteria in Dallas as the police, the secret service and other federal law enforcement authorities sought out the suspect who had evaded capture. Time evaporated as I continued my slow, dazed trek back toward the South Shore station where I could catch the train home to Indiana. Down in the lower lever of the station there was more screaming and commotion as televisions blasted out news of the killing. Everyone seemed dazed, unable to process what was happening. Police officers were crying and doing their best to comfort those in the station. I finally reached my train and stepped aboard realizing that I still had my ticket in my hand when I took my seat. It was not just me who walked pass the conductor; nobody had paid or handed over their tickets because the conductor had his face in his hands, crying unconsolably. It was a very long ride home.

Jonathan Kim

Episode 4: Payback

I made Jonathan angry one morning. I mean he was angrier than I had ever seen him. It was our usual practice to go to the water fountain and get a drink. And it goes without saying that he always filled his mouth with water and came after me. But I had the advantage because I could always catch him and squirt him back. But, on this day, he didn't seem to be in the mood for water play, still I chased him, caught him and sprayed him with water, getting him completely wet. He didn't appreciate it but there was not much he could do about it. For the remainder of our stay in the park, he moped around, not very playful and not wanting to talk to me. Other parents in the park had come to know us and they all noticed that Jonathan and I were not in our usual all-out playful mood and Jonathan's body language made it clear that he was quite unhappy about something. I apologized to him, but it did no good. He completely ignored me. I began to feel bad for having made him so angry. Soon it was time to leave the park and return to the cleaners. When we got back, Seon looked at Jonathan and just shook her head; she took him in the back, dried him off and changed his clothes as I took my seat in the front of the shop where I usually sat when waiting for him. Seon came back to the front first and we laughed about Jonathan's antics. Soon we were steeped in conversation. The more we talked, the better we understood one another, and we both enjoyed the interchange. Seon could see that I had genuine love for Jonathan. We laughed at something he had done and in the excitement of our levity I said, "I love Jonathan"! She stopped, looked at me and I could see a tear forming in her eye. As we spoke Jonathan came strutting from the back. He walked into the front of the shop and climbed over the low end of the counter and stopped right in front of me as I talked to his mother. Without any warning or expression of any kind, he shot a big spray of water directly into my face covering me from head to lap. I was totally soaked. He exploded in laughter as I sat there completely caught off guard, drenched, my face dripping. Seon gasped in shock; she couldn't believe what Jonathan had done to me right in front of her. I broke into laughter as I watched Jonathan. He had stepped back, jumping up and down in hysterics. Seon stood there dumbfounded, watching us. Jonathan had scored a direct hit. Good one, Jonathan! Good one!

The Other Denver Long

A Poem

I met a Greek teacher,
Whose last name was Long,
Her father, Denver,
Was big, bad, and strong,
We sent him my pictures
And I laughed 'cause I knew,
We'd never hear back
From that muffucka!

Buying Bush Beef

It wasn't long before Sam and Lammi, my housekeepers and translator schoolboys were running my house. And they did a damn good job. In the beginning Rick, my roommate and I put their honesty to the test and left small amounts of money and small "valuables" lying around. Watches and belts were of particular interest to kids from the village. Transistor radios were as good as gold. Rick and I would consult from time to time on the results and nothing ever came up missing. They became the true protectors of the house and we felt very comfortable with them. So, we 'adopted' them. Sam, the twelve-year-old and older of the two, talked to Rick and me like he was holding seminars. He always had talking points. The first thing we had to learn to do was to go down to the village on Fridays to get fresh 'bush beef'. That meant like six o'clock in the morning on Friday one of us would have to go down to the village about a quarter of a mile down the road and stake a claim to the fresh cut of meat we wanted from the butcher. Meat didn't get any fresher than 'bush beef'. So, I agreed to go to the village with Sam one morning to see how things were done. I was also interested in meeting the villagers. Sam beamed as we walked and ran down the road to the village and meandered through the throng of people milling about the marketplace. From time to time, Sam would bark out some Krio phrase and his friends would respond accordingly. Sam was introducing me to everybody as "Meestah Long from Chicago, Al Capone, Bang! Bang!"

The entire atmosphere of the marketplace was vibrant as the villagers engaged in enthusiastic conversations. I asked Sam where the butcher was, and he led me to a big crowd that stood surrounding some activity that I couldn't see from where I was. Sam weaved his way through the crowd with me in tow until we reached the opening. We stepped out of the thick crowd and into the opening just as the machete came crashing down. With one powerful blow, the cow's head fell to the ground, leaving the body standing for an instant. Blood gushed as if from a faucet. Then the legs folded, and the rest of the animal dropped to the ground like an anchor. It was a scene from *Apocalypse Now* where a villager beheads a cow. I had to catch my breath. Sam didn't tell me that we'd see a slaughter. He looked at me from a safe distance with a big grin on his face. He was anxious to see my reaction. I was holding it together as best I could until I turned away abruptly, choked a bit, and caught my breath. The cow had been completely beheaded only a few feet away, right in front of me. Sam laughed like crazy, and I wanted to kick his ass. Then the palavering (bargaining) started in earnest. Shouts in Mende, Temne and Krio abounded. The atmosphere was hyper as the villagers squabbled for which cut of the cow they wanted. The flies were in paradise. I was in hell, with

Sam. The scene looked like total confusion. But everybody knew exactly what they wanted as they left the area with paper bags, dripping blood, containing their fresh cuts of meat. In less than thirty minutes, there was little of the cow remaining. Sam bought a cut of the meat and promised me that I would like it when it was cooked properly. I had trusted Sam up to this point, but I didn't know about this time. After the visit to the butcher, I stepped way back from meat for a long time and made fish a main part of my diet. Back in the states if you wanted beef, you went to the market and bought it - already packaged. I was learning fast. I had taken for granted all the conveniences we had left behind at home, again.

While we were still getting settled, Rick and I decided that the house needed a good sweeping and cleaning out before the term started. The floors were concrete, so it was easy and safe to wash them down with heavy detergent and water and get behind every nook and cranny in the place. But when we started sweeping, the roaches started to come out. First there were a few. Then hundreds of roaches! And they were big roaches! They came from everywhere. The more we cleaned, the more they appeared. It was a scene from a Steven King horror movie. Rick and I were flabbergasted. Until we had started scrubbing the floors, neither of us had even seen a roach. I thought we had roaches in Chicago but they were nothing like these. These roaches could eat Chicago roaches. We had never seen anything like it. A three-inch roach was no big deal. Part of the problem too was that the roaches were too big to spray; that would have left an even bigger mess, so we fought the cleanup battle as best we could. Sam and Lammi were in hysterics, laughing throughout the entire ordeal, not lifting a finger to help. Sam told us in so many words that we got what we deserved by stirring them up. If we hadn't started cleaning with detergents, then the roaches would never have come out. They claimed we would never have seen them if we had left them alone. We dumped buckets of roaches soaked in kerosene. It was another lesson learned.

Soliloquy

A Face-to-Face Talk with Jesus

The year was 1971 and my mural design presentation to the Pilgrim Baptist Church of Rockford, Il. membership was an overwhelming success. The project was a 'go'. I was on my way to fame and fortune, I thought. At that final presentation something about the scale model caught my eye for an instant. It was a little thing, but it annoyed me. In the mural scene Jesus is on his knees from carrying the heavy cross; he is looking up at Simon, from Cyrene, a black man, who is lifting the cross. Simon, standing, is looking down at Jesus. Simon is above the halfway point in the mural. The scale model of the mural that American Olean Co. produced for me, when folded in half, folds right across the neck of Jesus. So, when the presentation was closed, the body of Christ is on the lower half and his head is on the upper half. How odd, I thought. I wondered why I had even noticed such a little thing like that. I moved on.

I wondered if I was making a negative cause for my life and creating some bad karma by working on a Christian church. I was a brand-new practicing Nichiren Buddhist chanting Nam-myo-renge-kyo. The current situation was

DENVER E. LONG BFA, MA, DPAKR

what I considered a test of my faith or just my lack of understanding. How odd indeed that my first professional job as a Black Buddhist industrial designer was a mosaic tile mural on a newly built Christian church.

I had done enough research in the Rockford, IL area previously to know the contractor that I was going the hire to do the construction. I chose Rockford Tile and Construction Company. For them my project was not their biggest job, but it was a very different, creative endeavor. They looked forward to the challenge. The mural was huge. It was a twenty by thirty-five feet. It was going to require over one hundred thousand one-inch square pieces of colored tile. It was a scene from the Bible. The scene shows Simone of Cyrene, who was ordered by the Roman soldiers to help Jesus, carrying the cross out of Jerusalem.

(*"And they compelled a passerby, Simon of Cyrene, who was coming in from the country, the father of Alexander and Rufus, to carry his cross."* Mark 15:21). Jesus, on his knees looks up at Simon in appreciation.

In my head the project was much more creative in its objective. It was about a young Black industrial designer bringing a congregation's vision to life right on the front of their brand-new church structure. The publicity gave both the Rockford Tile and Construction Company and American Olean Tile Company plenty of positive local news coverage. My legal paperwork was finally complete, and it was time for the construction to begin. As agreed, on a bright Monday morning, the construction company showed up at the sight and began building the enormous scaffolding. It took two days to complete the structure that went to the top of the church and covered the entire front of the building. It was a very exciting time for me and the members of the church. Before the work began, the workers installed a huge rolled up tarp at the top of the building. They were using the tarp to cover the design as they worked down the face of the building so that no one could see the design until it was unveiled in a ceremony some weeks away. I was like a kid in a toy store. No one was allowed near the work sight or scaffolding, except me. I was the boss, the chief honcho, I was 'The Man'.

The workers put in eight hours every day to complete the project on time and I was right there with them every day. I was even permitted to climb the scaffolding with the workers under the huge tarp. I could photograph the entire job from beginning to end, up close. I had never felt so in charge of anything even though I had nothing to do but take pictures and watch the professionals do their jobs. After a few days, the shadowed outline shape of the standing Roman guards in the mural began to take form. Then slowly Simon came into view, standing tall over Jesus. Days later, Jesus began to appear. By this time the workers were beginning to take a real interest in how the image was developing. They had seen the scale model, so their curiosity and excitement grew as everyone else's did. By the time the mural was about halfway down the front of the building, Jesus' face came into full form. Close up it was about eighteen inches from the top of his head down to his chin. My face was tiny in comparison. Jesus sported a gold halo. Then it occurred to me that I had been spending every day for a week, thirty feet off the ground on scaffolding, under a heavy tarp, looking directly into the face of Jesus Christ which was only inches away from mine. I decided to introduce myself:

"Good morning. I'm Denver; this is my project. I designed this mural. I'm a Buddhist. You know about Buddhism? What should I call you? Jesus of Nazareth? That's kinda formal don't you think? How about I call you something like Jes or Chris. Ok, Jesus of Nazareth it is. I'm Denver of Chicago. Chicago is in the new world. I don't think you'd know much about that. Anyway, just call me Denver. I used to read about you when I was a kid. To be honest, when I was a kid, I thought it was unfair that people said you could perform miracles, but that Santa Claus couldn't perform miracles. You know who I'm talking about? Sometimes they call him St. Nick. He was St. Nick of the North Pole. I always wanted to talk with you about him and get your input. But right now, Santa Claus is another story. What I really want to talk to you about is this situation you're in right now, you know, this crucifixion thing that's about to go down. I guess you realize by now that these folks plan to kill you. You do know that, right? And to demean you even more, they demand that you carry that damn cross. Now I can understand their beastly nature but what I can't understand is why you would oblige them. Why don't you refuse to carry that cross? What would they do if you refused to carry that cross? What, kill you? They're gonna do that anyway. I would respectfully decline and tell them to kiss my ass. But you don't curse, do you?"

"Check this out. I know a guy. He was in a situation just like yours, worse in fact. He was going to be beheaded by the powers that be, just like you. His name was Nichiren, Nichiren Daishonin. He was Japanese. You know about Japan? You couldn't know about him though because he's in your future and he's in my past so what I say is based on fact and evidence. Oh, to bring you up to date, this is the year 1971 and Nichiren lived in the thirteenth century. I think you'd like Nichiren. You two would have a lot to talk about. He's somebody I think you should know or at least know about. Check this out: Nichiren was a priest. Remember, he's in my past and in your future. Nichiren propagated the chanting of Nam-myoho-renge kyo, the Mystic Law of life or the Lotus Sutra. Unlike your teachings, he taught his disciples to praise and worship the Law-not him. And because of his activities, much like yourself, the authorities decided to execute him by beheading. Beheading was quick and one hundred percent effective. So in the dark of night, soldiers took him away to a former execution grounds, a beach, called 'Tatsunokuchi' and readied themselves for the execution. But unlike Simon who just helped lift the cross from your shoulder, Nichiren's disciple, a samurai named Shijo Kingo, vowed to die along with his mentor if the execution was carried out. How come nobody vowed to die with you like that? I often wondered about that. Nichiren declared to the heavens that no matter what, he would never forsake the Mystic Law. And just as the executioner raised his sword to behead Nichiren, the night sky lit up spectacularly from a meteor that streaked across the night sky. The event so scared the soldiers that they dropped their weapons and were afraid to carry out the execution. The executioner recoiled in fear. It seems that Nichiren was so in tuned with the universe that it extended its protection directly to him. Then as a gesture of profound compassion, Nichiren began encouraging the soldiers to chant Nam-myoho-renge-kyo and embrace the Mystic Law just as he had. What these Romans plan to do to you is going to be much worse than Nichiren's plight. What they plan to do to you is gonna hurt-a lot."

THE MEDIA

Seven days into the project word had gotten out and the news media were patrolling the neighborhood. Reporters began asking questions, taking pictures. They couldn't see anything because the heavy tarp covering the building was more than halfway down the wall. There were still about fifteen more feet of mural yet to go. The contractor let it be known how much they were enjoying the project. It made sense; I was generating business opportunities for them in the black church community. The minister was happy; the parishioners were happy; I was happy; everybody was happy. It was a great time to be happy! The church members told me how wonderful it was that I oversaw the project and that I was doing such a professional job. They all made assurances that I was certain to have a great career as a designer. By the time the final rows of tile were applied, the tarp had been dropped to the ground and nothing of the design could be seen. It was a ten-day project. Before the scaffolding came down the contractor, church members and I agreed on the unveiling date so that the local media could be notified.

On the Sunday afternoon of the unveiling, after church services, people from neighboring communities gathered out front. My mother was there, smiling from ear to ear. The local television station was there with reporters interviewing me and the people around me. It was without a doubt, my fifteen minutes of fame. When the mural was finally unveiled, there was an audible sigh of delight and a long round of applause. It was magnificent. The sun even began to shine directly onto the mural as if on cue. I could not have planned a more perfect unveiling. The project had been completed on time and on budget. There was an extended round of applause. From the very beginning, there had not been one hitch in the entire project. The pastor and the congregation all smiled at one another with their chests out as they continued to pat themselves and me on the back. The entire project from beginning to end went perfectly. It seemed impossible but it happened. My fifteen minutes of fame would not last long so I continued to bask in the attention for the rest of the week. In my mind I imagined new design contracts coming in from locations around the world: Vienna, Buenos Aires, and Milan, for starters. My name was going to be headline news in all the design publications around the world. I was 'tripping' like a big dog.

In Buddhism there is the principle of *"The Eight Winds"*:

"Worthy persons deserve to be called so because they are not carried away by the eight winds: prosperity, decline, disgrace, honor, praise, censure, suffering and

pleasure. They are neither elated by prosperity nor grieved by decline. The heavenly gods will surely protect one who is unbending before the eight winds." ("The Eight Winds" WND-1 794)

The wind of praise was like a hurricane. At the same time, I was placed right in the kind of job that I had chanted for. But for the previous ten days or so I had been spending some serious time with Jesus Christ, under a tarp. The entire project must have been karmic payback for all the bad stuff I had done in church. Maybe it was karma for the Welch's Grape Juice that I diluted when I worked at Delaney Memorial Methodist Church. Except for the spiritual confusion I felt, this first commission which was classified as an architectural design was an overwhelming success. Then, as suddenly as it had begun, it was over. My fifteen minutes of fame were over and done. Months went by and the church project still glowed as a bright memory in my mind.

Then one morning I got an urgent call from Rev. Gilbert at the church. They needed my help immediately regarding the mural. I called the contractors right away and they agreed to meet me at the church the next morning. I drove to Rockford to offer any assistance I could. During a recent severe storm in the area, lightning made a direct hit on the church. More specifically, the lightning bolt had struck the front of the church-the mural, like a bullseye. We all arrived at the church about the same time. When I saw the mural, I was stunned beyond belief. Lightning had clearly struck the mural directly; the black burn marks were visible from some distance away. To the architect, fire department captain and other authorities, it was not uncommon for high structures to be hit by lightning. To them it was just another lightning strike, until I pointed out something bizarre even to them. I went to my car and brought out the American Olean and Tile Company scale model of the design and opened the presentation model for them. Then I closed it and opened it several times to see if anyone noticed. Then suddenly one of the officials standing near me realized what had happened and exclaimed, "Well, I'll be damned!" Lightning had struck the mural dead center, vertically and horizontally, exactly corresponding to where the presentation model folded. The upper half of the mural was perfectly intact. Those one-on-one closeup conversations that I had had with Jesus crossed my mind and I began to wonder if these two things were connected. I specifically remembered telling Jesus about what the Roman soldiers were going to do to him. Exactly halfway down the mural, right where the model folded, was the head of Jesus. The lightning strike was so powerful that the lower half of the huge mural had slid right down the wall of the church into a neat pile on the ground, leaving the top half in perfect condition, beheading Jesus.

Santa of Rome

Life in Bunumbu remained normal until it was time to pack up for the last time. After two years, I was departing Sierra Leone from the same location, Lungi International Airport in Freetown. Travelers, coming and going, came through Lungi. At regular two-year cycles, new volunteers entered the country as old volunteers departed, making the city a hub of youthful activity. During these active days, Freetown was booming, especially at night. It was a time of travel for everybody. Those headed out were destined for places around the globe. When meeting someone new, the common question was: "Incoming?" This was the time when lots of news and information was being exchanged as everybody got to know everybody. Incoming volunteers brought news from home; the old volunteers brought news from the bush. For a week, parties abounded as the new volunteers headed to their posts up country. I was headed out. Word got around that I was an outgoing volunteer headed for Italy, destination Rome. I did not know that there was a Loyola University of Chicago campus in Rome. But many of the new, incoming volunteers had friends and even siblings at Loyola. They sought me out. If I would deliver some gifts to friends and relatives at the university in Rome, they would pay me. My air fare was already paid so anything else would be extra. We cleared the details and made a deal. Most of my personal belongings had already been sent ahead from Sierra Leone so I had only two pieces of luggage. The gifts were personalized with names and short messages from their senders but were mainly just African souvenirs. But the idea of my delivering a gift to a student in Rome who had a friend or relative in Sierra Leone was just too good to pass up. Now I not only had a destination, I also had a mission. I was going to Rome and play Santa Claus. The irony of my situation didn't escape me. I was going to deliver presents to little boys and girls who'd been good all year. I thought it would also be great if I could "get lucky" while I was in Rome because that was a very big and important part of my original dream.

I had planned my itinerary from Sierra Leone to Las Palmas in the Canary Islands to Rabat in Morocco, from there on to Lisbon, Portugal, then on to Spain. Many of us traveled together through to the Canaries and Morocco until we arrived in Spain. After Madrid, the group began to thin out as the destinations began to vary and some headed for home; others headed north and some remained behind in Spain. But I was going to cross the 'The Big Med', the Mediterranean Sea and head straight to Italy. From there I was headed back through, Paris, London, Amsterdam and maybe Antwerp.

Thinking back about an industrial design project in school at the Art Institute, a classmate had taken a color photo of his project, a beautiful wooden bench that he designed and built. When I saw that photo and how beautifully simple the shot was, it was then that I decided that one day I was going to buy myself a good reflex camera and Amsterdam was the place to do it. I was going to buy an Asahi Pentax 35mm camera, just like the one my pal used in school. I could get it from the duty free shop at Schiphol International Airport before heading back across the Atlantic Ocean for home. By the time I was ready to leave Madrid, I was really fired up because my next stop was Italy. I boarded an Alitalia airline, ready for the trip across the sea.

It was about nine o'clock at night as we descended into Fiumicino – Leonardo da Vinci International Airport also known as the Rome Fiumicino Airport. It was in Fiumicino about twenty miles southwest of Rome's historic city center. As I looked out the window on our approach, I noticed that there were water spots on the windows of the plane; it was raining. The view from the plane window looked like any other city at night. When we finally reached the gate and the plane's engines shut down, my heart started to pound rapidly. My heartbeat hastened as I left the plane and proceeded through the corridor to the luggage pickup. After a lengthy wait, the luggage finally started to drop from the carousel. I gathered my luggage and proceeded into the main corridor of the terminal building. Even at that hour of the evening the airport was bustling. I walked slowly as I drank in all the sights, sounds and smells of the airport. Instinctively I walked into the card shop. That's when the reality struck me. I was standing at a card case in the airport just outside of Rome, Italy. I was in my dream again only this time it was not a dream; it was real. It was night as I had imagined long ago and it was raining, something I loved. I was thinking that I must get a card sent home just like in the dream and I was alone in the airport, crying. Two nuns were in the shop, and they began to look at me as I stood there crying like a baby. Many years earlier, in my recurring dream about Rome, I would be standing at a post card stand in the Rome airport. It would be at night and raining. In the dream I worried that I must get a card sent home. I was not clear to whom to send the card but it still had to go out. I was alone and crying, not knowing what to do about the card. I was not afraid but frustrated and happy at the same time. There was a huge, bright cross hanging in the card shop and it annoyed me, having no obvious purpose in a card shop so I did my best to ignore it in the dream, but I couldn't. People stared at me as I stood there crying. They wouldn't stop staring at me. My feelings were mixed. I was angry. I was sad and I was happy all at the same time. Then I would wake up. I remembered the big cross in my dream. The cross had to represent the two nuns who stood there staring at me, not knowing what to do. It was no longer a dream. It was real. I was alive, in the airport in Italy, looking for just the right card to send to my father. I found a card and wrote: "Dear Dad, Need I say more? Love, Petie." Within minutes that card was out of my possession and on its way to the United States. I smiled as I strolled confidently through the terminal to the waiting buses outside. I had just made another of my life long dreams a reality.

Earlier in the summer, I had decided on a place to stay while I was in Rome. I rented a beautiful little apartment at the American Palace Eur Hotel, 554 Via Laurentina in the 'Jewish Ghetto' section of the city, near the city's famous Tiber River. It was located only a few yards from the metro train station. I thought the name was odd at first, but then I learned that 'ghetto' was not always in reference to the 'hood' back home. History showed that Jews had been isolated throughout Europe for many centuries, culminating in the German effort during WWII. It was a part of history. It was an immaculately clean apartment building and neighborhood. It felt like a cleaning service came every day and washed down everything: cars, buildings, streets, everything. I was amazingly comfortable in my little apartment, in ROME! It would have been nice to have an apartment like it back home. There were inner courtyards to the complex of buildings in the neighborhood where clothes lines ran from the side of one building to another. Clothes swayed back and forth in the warm breezes. Looking up from the ground was like looking through a painting, colorful and alive with musical movements of the freshly laundered clothes. They hung from the top floor all the way down to just above the lowest apartment. I quickly settled into my little apartment and began writing a letter. Back home my mother had bought colored push pins to place on the map that hung in my room. My nephew, *Sputnik*, Jo's son, was about ten years old and he was able to follow my travels by putting a push pin on the map for every location that I had mentioned in my letters. That map must have been colorful by now.

My first night's rest in Rome was complete. I slept like a tired teenager. The next morning was beautiful. It was warm and the sun shone brightly. After a big breakfast, I grabbed my bag loaded with the gifts and made my way to the Loyola University campus located on Mont Marie, the highest of the seven hills in Rome. I found myself gawking at all the sights along the way. Getting there was a challenge because on the way I realized that the drivers in Rome were the worse drivers on the planet. The traffic hurling around busy monuments and parkways were absolute suicide zones.

The sprawling Loyola campus was splendid. Immediately I could feel and see the effects of money, but I wasn't the least bit intimidated. I arrived on the campus at mid-morning and meandered around for a short time until I came up on a group of students who seemed relaxed, standing around talking and laughing. These were all rich kids. None of them had to worry about the U.S. draft. Money had secured them safely away on campuses and private schools around the country. I approached them, introduced myself and explained that I had just arrived in Rome the day before from Sierra Leone, West Africa as a U. S. Peace Corps volunteer. The students perked up when I told them that. As soon as they realized that I was an American Peace Corps volunteer, the conversation lit up and got energized. They had questions for me about living in Africa. I had questions for them about living in Rome. We talked for an hour and then after giving them some of my experiences, I explained to them why I was in Rome, at Loyola University. As I spoke, I took out my list of names of the students for whom I had brought gifts. When they heard this, there was a small uproar, finding it hard to believe that I had come all the way from Africa to deliver gifts to them and some of their friends. It blew their minds. As I began to read off the names, two students, a young lady and young man both shouted out, "That's me! That's me!" Within the hour, word had spread around the campus that a guy was there to deliver presents from Peace Corps friends and relatives in West Africa. I was an instant celebrity. If Dad could see me now. I flashed back to the conversations I had had with him when I promised him that when I got to Rome, the people were going to love me and take me in. These were rich kids and I was their special guest. They took me into one of the buildings on campus and created a private party atmosphere where I read off the rest of the names and handed each student their present along with a personal note from the sender. By late in the evening I had met every student whose name was on the list and dozens more. One of the students for whom I had brought a gift was a gorgeous young lady from California. She was petite with short, dark hair, almost black; she owned big brown eyes that oversaw a body the color of ginger. She had a tan that could only have come from lying in the sun, a lot. In my mind she looked like a tiny version of Liz Taylor. She even had a mole on her face. She is the girl I saw in my childhood fantasies.

The most remarkable and outstanding thing about her appearance were her lips; they were a burning hot red. I couldn't tell if it was from lipstick or wet paint but her lips captivated me. I wanted to kiss her, right there, on the spot. And not stop there. How could a girl be so beautiful and talk to me? Her name was Candy. I recalled a paperback book about a little vixen with fire red lips whose name was

Candy, but this one was real. When I told Candy where I was living, she told me to move out and live on campus with them for free until I left the country. It must have been love at first sight with Candy and me because less than an hour later, I was riding merrily through the streets of Rome in the back seat of a red convertible sports car with not just one, but two beautiful, rich young American women/ students. Candy was driving and one of her girlfriends, Lisa, was riding shotgun. If only Dad could see me now. It was really happening. During the ride through town, my mind wondered back to the days at home when I boasted to my father about the day I'd go to Rome and be welcomed and how I'd have mad, passionate love affairs with beautiful women in exotic places around the world. As I lay back, looking at all the sights, I was thinking that this ride through the streets of Rome was a good start.

Once I moved into a dorm room on the campus, Candy and I became an instant item. Until then I had never thought of myself as a particularly desirable guy, not like Lou was. I was short, medium brown with a healthy, trim physique. I was in good shape with an even brown complexion that boasted of caramel and I had a 'six pack'. But according to Candy, what she and the other girls found sexy about me were my muscular legs. I had muscular legs from having spent so much time at the skating rink as I was growing up. All those afternoons at the rink were finally paying dividends. I had to admit that for my size, my legs were impressive, so I made it a point to always wear shorts.

Candy's father was a big shot American diplomat in Rome. Back home he owned some big financial enterprise;

he was a multi-millionaire. Candy had been in Rome for over a year, studying political science. Both her mother and father lived in a high rise building in an exclusive part of town. In one of our conversations, I asked Candy what her parents would think if they knew she was with a black guy. She laughed embarrassingly and assured me that they would not take kindly to the idea. Then I realized why she was doing it. I suspected it was out of spite toward her parents. I thought that if Candy wanted to be with me just to spite her parents, then I say, "Cool, who I am to interfere in family matters?" She told me that she didn't always do what her parents wanted her to do. I was happy to hear that. Then it was deja-vu all over again. I asked why she would even want to date a black guy around all her little rich white friends. She blushed and her laughter gave me my answer. In her world I must have represented the gold standard of taboos. And I had just come straight out of Africa!

Once I hooked up with the male students, I spent very little money. They fed me, took me to parties and showed me all the fun spots in the city to check out while they were in class. Candy and I went to the Coliseum together making a quick getaway from the group for some private time together. Reality check: It was me, Denver E. Long, sitting in the coliseum in Rome, Italy taking pictures with my date, the most beautiful girl I have ever known. And just like in my fantasies---she wants me!!! I was dizzy with the impact of my realization. So much so that Candy asked if I were ok. I was just fine.

I was a part of the group for nearly a month. The night before my departure, the students planned a big going away party for me at, of all places, Candy's parents' high-rise apartment. Departure day finally arrived. I was really concerned about causing a problem and losing my ass. But I was assured by Candy that they were out of the country on business travel and had left the apartment to her even though she spent all her time on campus. She always had access to the luxury apartment but spent little time there when her folks were in town. The apartment was on an upper floor of a high rise building; it boasted a balcony that overlooked the sprawling city below. At the party, I was the guest of honor. I was looking very dapper and proper, dressed completely in white. My outfit had been provided by one to the students whom I had brough a present from Sierra Leone. My linen shirt and trousers were so white that I looked aglow. The party was controlled but crazy; everybody was having a great time. To me it was all magical.

Standing next to me on the balcony was Candy; she was wearing a very tiny, very thin, very red dress that matched her very red lips. It looked like red paint, and I was ready to smear it. If ever there was a scene in a movie where a little vixen was displaying all her assets, this was it. If I touched her, I'd burn my fingers. If I rubbed against her, I'd sizzle. She was on fire. I was on fire. I was fantasizing about all the nasty things that I wanted to do to her when The Beatles sang out: *"Hey, Jude"* and that moment etched itself into my memory. The music was mesmerizing. Together Candy and I silently looked out over the city of Rome at night and then at each other. It was lust at first sight.

"Hey, Jude, don't make it bad. Take a sad song and make it better. Remember to let her into your heart. Then you can start to make it better, better, better, better!"

Did I say it was magical? I was again in a short-term relationship that would end very soon. We both acknowledged that we'd probably never meet again. We stood there silent for a long time, eyes fixed on one another, enjoying the perfect moment. We hadn't touched yet, but we could both feel the heat. And though I had argued with my dad to the contrary, this moment was perfect. We partied late. When the party was finally over and everyone had left, as she had planned, Candy and I were alone until morning. Life was good.

A few days before I left Rome, I was able to call Didier Alann in Paris and let him know that I would be in France in a few days. He sounded excited and delighted. I left Rome smiling, having fulfilled another dream. What more could the future have in store, I wondered. Life is what you make of it. I spent the next month traveling through Europe with Didier. He was my guide and protector while I was in Paris. I stayed with him and his brother in a small, very classy and fashionable apartment. We could see the Arch de Triumph in the distance from where they lived. It was right in the heart of town, where they assured me "all the action is." They were right. After a month, I was worn out and ready for some rest, something I could not get in Paris. So, I decided it was time to move on. My new camera was in Amsterdam waiting for me.

It appears the stars were all aligned because I phoned Rita in Antwerp, Belgium and got her on the telephone with the first try. When she realized who it was on the line, she started screaming. I was screaming, too. I told her that I was on my way back home to the states, but on my way, I was stopping for sure in Amsterdam to get my camera and stop in Brussels. She sounded shell shocked on the phone, repeating that she never thought I would call her in a million years, but here we were, again. We were both excited about the chance to see each other again. During the conversation, I realized that it would be better if we both met in Amsterdam since Brussels was between Paris and Amsterdam, otherwise I'd be making two stops. But that was a lot to be hoping for. It would be such an imposition to ask her to fly to another country just to meet me. The flight time is only a few hours but still I didn't impose. As it turned out I didn't have to impose; things were getting better and better. Rita and Anna, whom Lou and I had met in Las Palmas, were themselves headed for Amsterdam the next day! It seemed that Anna's sister, Marie, the medical student, was going to be in Amsterdam with some of her friends from school for just a few days and demanded that Anna and Rita come and meet them there. Rita and Anna were leaving the next morning. So was I. The timing was perfect. Ahead of time, Rita warned me that we might not be able to get together until the second day because of some big private party that she and her sister's friends were committed to attending. It was a big dance party celebration for their first night in Amsterdam, so they had promised to attend. That was fair. Two days together instead of three would still be great. At the last minute, Didier decided to come to Amsterdam with me. That was a big benefit, and I was joyous. He had been to Amsterdam many times before and knew the city. He also spoke some Dutch. When we arrived at Schiphol International, we went directly to the Hotel Corona at De Lairessestraat 11 in Amsterdam where I had reserved a room before we left Paris. Didier even split the cost. He was a real treasure to be with and I felt safe with him. There was no fear in him. If he wanted to do something, he did it. He reminded me of Fred back home. Once we had settled into our room, Didier got on the phone and got so involved in several conversations, in several languages, that I thought for a moment that he was a native of Amsterdam. For him everywhere was home. Again, I was impressed. He had planned our first night out in Amsterdam, but first we ate and rested. It was about six o'clock p.m. We took his advice and after a hearty meal, we both crashed. We awoke around ten o'clock. I felt refreshed and ready to party. Once we showered and changed clothes, we headed for a night out. I followed Didier everywhere. I wondered what I would have done had I come alone. I felt good, invigorated and excited to be in another exotic country with all kinds of new people, especially girls.

The city was alive. There was activity in every direction. At a coffee shop we met the young folks from Amsterdam that Didier had been talking to on the telephone. They were good hearted and very friendly. I was introduced as Didier's friend and guest from the United States who had just come from living in Africa. He made me sound like Albert Schweitzer. From that moment on, I was part of the group. From the coffee shop we all headed to a party. Two of the guys in the group had cars so we piled into each and headed for the celebration held at an open air venue a few miles from where we were. We could hear the music from some distance away as we approached the action. There were hundreds of people dancing and singing and just having a wonderful time. It was a world peace party. Just then Didier said, "Ok, let's party!", as he led me and the group into the festivities. It looked like every part of the world was represented in the crowd. I could hear different languages as we headed through the crowd. There was an upbeat atmosphere enveloping the entire crowd. I followed Didier as he wove his way further and further into the crowd. Earlier in the day he told me that if we were lucky and he could locate them, I'd get a chance to meet some girls from Paris that he knew. Then from a distance he yelled out a name to someone ahead of him in the crowd. She was a beautiful young blonde. They greeted each other and hugged vigorously as they got reacquainted. They laughed about something in Dutch. After a few more moments of kissing and hugging Didier turned and introduced me to the young lady. She gave out a big smile as she came over and hugged me so tightly that I was caught completely off guard. Her name was Helga, and she was one of Didier's ex-girlfriends. Now we were following Helga through the crowd to find her group of girlfriends. There were girls everywhere, of every color, size, nationality, of every description, speaking every language. I was in party paradise. Suddenly Helga shouted out to a group of a dozen or so young women ahead of us and they all turned to see us approaching. And to my utter astonishment, standing right in the middle of about twelve or thirteen girls was Rita. Our eyes met; both of our mouths dropped open as we froze. We both stood there in absolute shock and awe, staring right into each other's faces, tears beginning to run down her face. Without a word being said, we grabbed each other and embraced for a long moment. Several times we stepped back from one another to look at each other's face and then hugged again. By now the rest of the group was standing there with their mouths agape, speechless, looking at Rita and me, not knowing what was happening. After a few seconds Didier must have remembered our meeting in Las Palmas and he explained it to the rest of the group. Didier had met Rita and Anna when we were in Las Palmas. We never thought we'd be at the same party. Just like in Las Palmas, Rita and I spent the next three days together until it was time for us both to leave Amsterdam. Like so many other times in the past, I knew, and Rita knew that we would never see each other again but that was ok.

From the time I left home up until the day I left the continent of Europe heading back home, I had 'fallen in love' every time my planes landed. I counted at least six landings. I had forgotten to be careful what I wished for. My attitude whenever I met a new girl was, 'just take me'. It worked. I left the Netherlands with a smile on my face and more precious memories in my heart. Out of all the excitement and merriment that I experienced, there was something deeply comforting about the fact that I was just an ordinary person fulfilling one dream after another based solely on faith. I imagined what I could have done if I had had real talent or dare say, lots of money. But that was exactly the point. I wish I could take credit for saying it first but: "If I can do it, anybody can do it". I gained a degree of understanding about life, mankind, and the workings of the universe. Suddenly I understood the mystery of the universe. It was all so simple. It all boils down to three words: lots of sex. As I saw it life was wearing white or maybe red silk panties.

On the day of my flight back to the U.S. I bought my first 35mm reflex camera. As planned, I bought a 35mm Asahi Pentax and I was ecstatic.

Jonathan Kim

Episode 5: Double Dog Dare

Jonathan was an excellent reader and he loved books. One of our favorite hangouts was the kids' section of the bookstore just a few doors down from my office on the corner of Kimbark and 57th Street. We spent hours, sitting on the floor downstairs reading to each other, sometimes buying books that Jonathan thought he could not live without. Whenever I bought Jonathan a book out of my pocket Seon would insist that she pay me back. I always refused. The owner and staff at the bookstore knew Jonathan and me from our regular visits. They would bring us new books to check out.

One of our favorite games was to dare one another to do something silly. He would dare me, and I would dare him back. If you ever got a Double Dog Dare challenge, that was the biggest dare of all. To turn down a 'DDD' meant that you were a 100% "chicken". You clucked like a chicken; you walked like a chicken, and you looked like a chicken. In short, you were chicken through and through!

In the bookstore one Saturday morning I saw a chance to really get even with Jonathan and blow his mind at the same time. On our way out of the bookstore, there was woman police officer standing near the front counter with her back to us. She was reading a magazine and she had no idea we were behind her, so I dared Jonathan to go up to the officer, tap her on the shoulder and give her a big hug. "Are you crazy!!!" he shouted at me. That was the absolute craziest thing he had ever heard. So, I double dared him. "No way!!" he declared. Then I applied the pressure and Double-Dog Dared him. I clucked at him: "Cluck! Cluck"! I threatened to tell everybody that Jonathan feared a Double-Dog Dare. He refused and I laughed and made fun of his "chicken feathers". Then he did exactly what I knew and expected him to do: he dared me to do it. I hesitated, pretending to be thinking about it. Then he double dared me, and finally he Double-Dog Dared me. I continued to hesitate so that he would think he had me on the ropes. He began to cluck at me, so I accepted his dare. I slowly walked up to the officer, tapped her on the shoulder and walked around her to face her as I put my arms around her and hugged her. She returned the hug. As I looked back over her shoulder at Jonathan, I could see him standing there, mouth open, staring at me with the look of absolute disbelief on his face. He stood there motionless, mouth open, staring. When I let go of the officer, I stepped around her and walked back over to Jonathan who was speechless and in awe of me. He could not believe what I had just done. I never said a word. I just ushered him toward the door so that we could leave the bookstore. I was laughing inside but I pretended to be calm as I opened the door for Jonathan to exit. What he didn't know was that I had already recognized the officer as one of my clients and when I stepped in front of her, I told her that my little friend Jonathan was behind her and that he dared me to hug her. So, I asked her not to turn around but pretend that we were strangers. She complied and as we hugged, we laughed; I explained to her what Jonathan was going through as he stood behind her staring at us. He was clearly in awe of me. We sent Jonathan's mind into the outer limits of space. Good one, Denver. Good one.

The Big Race

Life was good living in the bush. Every day was a joy, especially since my "adopted son', Sam had provided me with an unlimited supply of prime yamba (ganja). He encouraged me to "Pick your proper time and smoke yamba! It tis for your true enjoyment, Meestah Long." I especially appreciated his keen, mature sense of humor. Sam was a twelve-year-old bush kid and a survivor who deserved my respect; and I gave it to him. Sharp-witted and curious, we talked about overcoming obstacles and the challenges that life presented, real serious stuff. Our biggest challenges were physical. Our mental challenges were another story. It all boiled down to which of us was the most physically fit. All the kids thought Americans were fat and lazy. I showed him different, hence our competitive relationship quickly developed. Sometimes he won; sometimes I won. I was in top physical condition, so I'd take on all of his challenges and he was very good at physical feats. He did live in a village in the bush. My mind shot back to the very good practical jokes that he had pulled on me. Fresh in my mind was the surprise slaughter scene in the village that he intentionally led me to, when I first arrived in-country.

Then there were the roaches that my roommate and I tried to rid the house of. Sam laughingly let us know that if we had left them alone, they would not have been a problem. He refused to help. There was also the time Sam laughed at me for being gay because my male students held my hand. At the time I didn't know it was a custom for male friends to hold hands. Sam didn't tell me that; instead, he pretended I was on the queer side. He enjoyed that little stunt a lot; he even told his little friends about how uninformed I was. I was a good sport about it all. Besides it was funny, even to me. My great appreciation goes to him for providing me with his own specially grown cannabis. The best weed in the world.

This time Sam and I were playing for big stakes: new sneakers and five Leones ($5.00)-cash. When the stakes finally reached the new sneakers level, Sam got serious. To Sam and the other kids in the village, getting a new pair of white sneakers was more valuable than anything. Promise a kid some white sneakers and they would do anything for an employee. The sneakers were so precious that they were only worn on special occasions. Everyday footwear was either sandals or barefoot.

The big event was that I challenged Sam to race me from our front door to my art building. It took me about ten minutes to walk the distance. It was about one and a half city block in distance, but the path was through bush, up inclines, etc. If I ran at top speed, I could make it in about five minutes. I made him an offer he couldn't refuse. The challenge was that the first one of us to reach my building wins. If I win, Sam works for free for a week. If he wins, he gets a new pair of sneakers and five Leones. He was chomping at the bit. I could not have made the offer more tantalizing. Sam was like a wild stallion, exuding energy, raring to run, to go. He was so ready.

At the starting line, we stood back-to-back at the front doorstep waiting for the count down. We faced off in directions that opposed the direction of the art building. I wanted to assure Sam that this way neither of us would have the advantage. He agreed. "On your mark! Get set! Go!". Sam was gone! He was gone! Disappeared! I could just barely hear the bushes rustle as he flew through the bush. I could imagine the energy and determination that was being released by him as he tore through the growth. There was no way I could beat him to my studio and I knew it. Sam should have known. Amazed at Sam's speed, I chuckled, turned and went back inside the house. I went straight to my stash box and rolled a joint the size of Sharpie pen. It was the most beautiful joint I had ever seen. I took a beer from the refrigerator and headed for the front porch. *Christo Redentor* by Donald Byrd was coming in from the BBC. I propped myself back in my big chair, popped my brew and fired up. After about fifteen minutes, I was zoomin' when I heard footsteps. It was Sam stepping out of the bush, looking down as he approached. I guessed that it took him fifteen minutes to realize that I wasn't coming. We looked at each from across the short distance as I sat back with my legs extended and crossed enjoying my beer, and nearly hidden in a cloud of yamba smoke. No words were uttered. At that moment he could read my mind:

"Pick your proper time and smoke yamba! It tis for your true enjoyment, Meestah Long."

I laughed until I left Sierra Leone. "Good one, Meestah Long. Good one."

Margaritas

Some years ago, my wife and I took our first trip to Cancun, Mexico. We were two excited novices, anxious to explore the sights, sounds and night life of Mexico. We had travelled to many other places, but Mexico was new. Our plane landed at Cancun International Airport early in the morning which gave us another full day of explorations and excitement. By noon we had checked into our hotel room and unpacked the few light weight things that we brought. Neither of us could wait to see the city and the sights so we freshened up and left the room with big expectations. When we reached the beautiful lobby of the hotel, we noticed that it was very quiet; there was hardly any activity. We had to adjust our eyes as we stepped off the elevators into the bright open lobby. Our sunglasses would be needed outside in that brilliant sunlight. There were no tourists or others standing at the counter. As we approached the front desk there was only one clerk behind the counter. She was a young lady whose name was easy for me to remember; it was Maria. Joan asked Maria directions for specialty stores and restaurants. They chatted pleasantly for a few minutes, laughing from time to time as Maria handed Joan a sheet of paper or brochure on how to get where she wanted to go.

We proceeded to the front entrance and the glaring rays of the sun. Our sunglasses came out. We were ready. Under the large canopy just outside the hotel entrance were two young men who greeted us politely as we stepped under the canopy. "Hola", they said as we came closer. "Hola", we responded. Both men wore hotel uniforms: both smiled; both were named Jose. We all laughed. It was their jobs to make sure all new hotel arrivals had their luggage properly handled and carried to the rooms. Through our broken Spanish and the two Jose's' broken English, we understood them when they wished us a good day. The duo looked at us then at each other quizzically as we turned to leave. They were clearly puzzled by our request and intentions. "Adios," they said simultaneously as we strolled away. Joan and I laughed as we turned and stepped into the bright sunlight. It was hot! We scampered across the completely empty and quiet street to the other side and started walking down the beautiful boulevard. Nothing moved. We walked and as we passed a hotel with diners sitting in the windows, they looked out at us and shook their heads as we went by. We found our restaurant. The time was exactly one thirty. The restaurant was beautiful, and we could see immediately why people would want to eat there. The items on the posted menu made my mouth water. The restaurant was also closed. The sign said in Spanish and English: "Closed from 1:00pm-3pm for siesta." It didn't take us long to "get it". That sign explained everything. No wonder the streets were quiet and the Josses were puzzled and laughing at us-dumb Gringos. Everybody takes a nap during hottest part of the day. Even animals in the wild knew that. We looked at each other with the same thought: "Dahhhhh!!!!!!"

Later in the evening after we had returned to our room, eaten and rested sufficiently, we showered and set out to party. Again, we imposed on the front desk for directions to the best party spots or bars or dance halls or wherever the "action" was. The only challenge was that to get to where the action was, we would have to take a bus. The hotel would provide a ride there, but we'd have to take the city public bus back. The hotel bus left twice every evening. The nine o'clock bus was the last one to leave the hotel. We got that one. The ride took about ten to fifteen minutes and when we got off, it was like a different world. Bars and restaurants lined both sides of the street for blocks. It reminded us of Vegas. There was music, laughter, and lots and lots of people, primarily tourists. The night was alive with revelers. It was clear to me that we were right in the middle of the tourists' play pen. There were people from everywhere; you see it in their dress; you could hear it in their languages. The one thing everybody had in common was partying and having a good time. It was hard to decide which bar to visit since there were so many. We decided to pick one that was just one flight up from the sidewalk and overlooked all the action on the bustling street below. Many of the bars had an open balcony. Most of the bars were crowded; from the sidewalk below, you could look up and see the patrons dancing and celebrating. Neither Joan nor I wanted to go into a place that was too crowded, so we picked one less congested.

The bar we chose, Le Hacienda was empty. It was a spacious, open area with a balcony that overlooked the busy street below. We were the only patrons in the entire place; music was playing softly in the background. We sat next to the railing on the spacious balcony. Joan and I looked at each other wondering why the place was so dead. Just then a young woman who appeared to be in her early thirties came over to our table to take our order. "Hola", I said. She replied, "Hola"! With a big smile she asked in unaccented English, "What will you have?" I responded, "Margaritas". Again, she smiled and said, "Two margaritas coming up". Shortly the drinks came, and we stared at them because they were huge. We made a toast and decided that they were the best margaritas either of us had ever had. As we got comfortable with our choice of venue and libation, I got an idea. I shared it with Joan and we both agreed to put it into action. When the waitress noticed that our glasses were getting low, she came back to the table to serve us. "What's your name?", I asked. The young woman smiled again and said, "My name is Joan", she responded. "WHAT!!!!! "My name is Joan. My wife's name is Joan," we shouted out simultaneously. "What are the chances? My name is Denver", I continued. They laughed together and bonded immediately. "We're from Chicago, down here to have a little party fun.", I added. "Denver and Joan are from Chicago. I like that. My husband, Tony and I own the bar and restaurant. We're both from California. His folks still live here in Mexico; mine are still in the States, in Maryland. My last name is now Torres; it used to be Simon, she told us. "From now on, I'm going to call you JT so that everybody will know who I'm talking to and about. Ok? "Ok", she agreed. 'How long have you guys been living here in Mexico?", I asked.

They had just begun their second year as bar/restaurant owners but had been living in Mexico for the last twelve years. The first year for the business was spent getting licensed, paying taxes, getting all the legal documents in order and stocking the place with supplies. It helped that Tony's dad had some connections in Cancun. So far, they had not made any money with the business because finding the right employees had also been a real challenge. So far, they had only one employee, Emily, who helped with all the different responsibilities. With only one employee on the payroll, they were now ready to get the ball rolling. JT called her husband over to our table and introduced him to us. JT introduced us with: "This is Joan and Denver from Chicago." His name was Tony, and he immediately caught the names of the two women and laughed. Tony was a handsome guy in his early forties who quickly extended his hand to shake. I told him that he looked like one of my favorite old Hollywood movie stars named Gilbert Roland. Noted for his dashing good looks, Roland, a Mexican, was twice nominated for a Golden Globe award. What really made Tony smile was when I informed him that Gilbert Roland was just the actor's screen name. Roland's real name was Luis Antonio Damaso de Alonso. In short, his name was Tony, too. We laughed. "JT and Tony T", I said. When she heard it, she laughed aloud and explained to her husband what the joke was as they turned and walked back to their duties. The young couple wished us an enjoyable visit and to let them know if we needed anything else; they would personally attend to it.

When JT and Tony came back to the table, I put my idea out to them. "We noticed that we're the only customers. I suppose your competition up and down this strip is ferocious, especially during the hot tourist season," I said. They confirmed that the more established bars had reputations that brought them a lot of business, but still they were newcomers. "Ok, guys, this is my idea: for every two people that we get to come up here, we get one free margarita! Two for one. What do you think?", I said. They paused for a moment, looked at each other and in unison said, "Deal!" They left our table laughing and talking excitedly as they returned to their duties. Joan and I worked on our margaritas as we discussed our strategy for winning free drinks for the rest of the night. First, we would have to be sufficiently 'lubricated' to attain the necessary state of mind to carry out the plan. Second, we would have to be enjoying ourselves so much that others would want to come up and join us. That means music-good, loud, danceable music. Third, a costume. Tony said we were welcomed to wear the sombreros that were hanging throughout the large open space. With my large hanky around the neck and the sombrero, I had a costume. Joan donned one, too.

On request, Tony turned up the music so that it could be heard downstairs, on the street, like the other bars. It didn't take long for Joan and me to start feeling frisky, so we got up and started dancing. We were feeling the margarita and the music do their thing on us. For just the two of us, we were getting pretty loud as we sat, drank and looked over the balcony to the sidewalk below. "Chicago!" I shouted to a couple passing below us. "Montreal!", came the reply. "Neighbor!", I replied. "Come up and join us, neighbor!" And they did. I introduced them to Joan and then to JT who was surprised to see guests coming in so soon after I had made my deal. His name was Carl, and her name was Karen, both from Montreal. They were enjoying college break and had just arrived in town a few hours earlier. This was their very first night stop. Carl was big guy; I figured he played football. He was a second-year medical student at the University of Michigan. Karen was the educator; she was working on her PhD in Montreal. It had been difficult for them to be together because of their schedules so this trip had to count. I offered them a sombrero, and they both accepted. They took the table right next to ours and within minutes the four of us were drinking margaritas, dancing, and shouting over the railing at tourists and other passersby. Tony came over to the table, smiled at us and said, "Wow!" We had just received our first free margarita. From the time Carl and Karen joined us, the party only got bigger and livelier.

The place was getting more activity as those we encouraged started to encourage others to come up. In no time the young couple had gotten into the spirit of the party and started shouting out cities over the railings. "Brooklyn", someone shouted from below. In perfect unison, everybody near the balcony responded with: "Brooklyn"! The idea had caught fire. "Miami"! By the first hour, every sombrero from the walls were now perked atop some patron's head. "San Francisco"! JT, Tony, and Emily were busier than they had ever been. And with every new couple that came up and joined us, there was another margarita added to out table. "Boston"! ~ The shoutouts went on all night. The place was jumpin'. "Memphis"! At one point a couple that had come up to join us said that they had just left another bar to come here. She said that word was going up and down the street that there is a special party going on. We just plucked people off the street. "London"! Within two hours the place was packed. Everybody was dancing, having one good time. I couldn't believe how many people we had gotten to come up and fill the big empty space. Tony and JT were flabbergasted. "Amsterdam"! Not only did they have a busy night, but they also found a young woman in the crowd who had somehow impressed Tony so much that he offered her a job while she was out of school. There were folks from everywhere in the party and they were not bashful about dancing. At last count I had earned twelve free margaritas. "Copenhagen"!

Jonathan Kim

Episode 6: Four in a Row

Every time Jonathan and I took a jaunt, he never failed to do something unexpected and/or hilarious that usually left me in stitches. I learned early on to carry my camera with me whenever I was out with him. I always looked forward to the little excursions that we took together, each time going further and further from the office and his mother. As the months rolled into our first year, Jonathan and I grew very close. Some weekends he went with me to buy wood for my fireplace at home. He always loaded one and only one log into the trunk of the car. We spent the entire day together until it was time for the cleaners to close then I'd take back to the cleaners. Whenever he talked to his mother about my wife, Joan, he always referred to her as "Denver's mom." I don't' know what that was about. No matter how she tried to get him to understand who she was, he still referred to her as my mom. It was hilarious.

By the time Jonathan was six years old, he was as much a part of my life as my office and business were. It was not unusual for him to come running into my office to tell me something he had discovered or something new that his mother had taught him. He had a desk in my office with his back to the window so that his mother could look in and check on him without him ever knowing she was there. She could see me, and I could see her; it was our little secret that we kept from Jonathan. He was set up with paper and markers that he could use any time he came into the office. It was clear that Seon felt amazingly comfortable with Jonathan being with me so much. She told me that he was fortunate to have such a good friend. I assured her that it was I who was fortunate to have Jonathan as a friend. Either way we both knew that Jonathan and I loved one another; she was very happy about that. Clients who came into my office began asking about Jonathan if they didn't see him sitting at his desk busily turning out one drawing after another. One third of the clients who met him did so by accident. It was usually when he came running into the office, excited about something. Bank customers and passersby considered him a part of my business. He had a thing for drawing the same thing over and over; it was usually some kind of bug or insect. I suggested, "Jonathan, why don't you try to draw something different. Draw me"! I spoke. He immediately got to work. He did not look at me one time when he did his drawing; he just started drawing. It took him only a few minutes and then he said, "Ok, here. This is you"! When I looked at his drawing, I was both impressed and flattered. It was a simple stick figure drawing depicting me. It was amazingly accurate, and it presented me with my roundish framed glasses, my baseball cap but most importantly, it showed me with a big smile on my face. Across the drawing was my name: "D e N v E r".

Jonathan had a fascination with the plastic sign that hung on the glass entry door to the office. It let customers know when I would return; the other side gave office hours. The sign was attached to the glass with a suction cup. When you promise something to a kid, they do not forget! Ever! And they won't let you forget either. Jonathan knew that when my office closed at noon on Saturday the rest of the day belonged to him. Lunch always came first; usually pizza then we were off on some new adventure. It was our regular lunch time, but I had to take care of a last-minute client. I was at my desk, talking with the client. Jonathan was at the door, behind the client but facing me. My attention was torn momentarily between what I was saying and what he might do at any moment. Slowly and deliberately, he pulled the suction cup off the glass, spit in it and slammed it into the middle of his forehead, allowing the sign to drop, completely covering his face. It was all I could do the avoid laughing out loud while my client was facing me. But I failed miserably and when she realized I was being distracted, she turned around only to see a little boy standing in the middle of the office with a baseball cap turned around backward on his head and his face completely covered with my office sign, reading, "12:00 Out to Lunch". Good one, Jonathan.

Every Saturday was a day of joy and laughter for me, hanging out with Jonathan. I loved every minute of it. Our regular breakfast/lunch hangout was Salonica's restaurant on 57th St., about four blocks away from the office. We ventured further and further away every week. But Salonica's was so much our 'home' that the waitresses knew exactly what Jonathan would order and he never disappointed. Our favorite waitress, Erin, was so accustomed to his antics that they would often get into arguments like two adults. On this day the restaurant was more crowded than usual. There were people even lined up waiting to get in. But Jonathan and I were already in our spot waiting for our food. There was a lot of commotion on the other side of the restaurant and voices were murmuring much louder than usual. Who or whatever was causing the stir was coming on our side of the restaurant. As the new arrivals came in and found their seats, the other voices in the restaurant softened again as everyone returned to eating. Jonathan became annoyed because he didn't get what he had ordered. Erin, who always waited on us, had taken our orders but for whatever reason everything came back wrong. Jonathan said to her, "I asked for Fruit Loops; you know I always order Fruit Loops and you brought me corn flakes. I asked for grape juice and you brought me orange juice. Denver ordered raisin toast and you brought him wheat toast. What is the problem this morning? Are you having a bad day? You should go lie down and take a rest break", he continued. Erin scowled at me, then at Jonathan and shot back, "What are you now-my therapist? You know it's not every day that I get a chance to seat and serve the next President of the United States," she explained. I laughed out loud at her frustration and congratulated her on her good fortune. Jonathan didn't get it. He had no idea who Senator Barack Obama was.

From Salonica's we headed for the grocery store to pick up items for Jonathan's mom. The store was even further away from the office but our walk became another adventure; we talked and laughed along the way, Jonathan sparking conversations with most strangers we passed. Many were surprised at his openness and happy demeanor. People looked upon us as the odd couple, a black guy and a Korean kid who act like playmates rather than adult and child. I must admit that when we were together, I was a child again. We reached the grocery store and I went right to the produce department to pick up Seon's items. I turned around and Jonathan was gone. In a momentary panic, I rushed back to the entrance of the store and there he was, just standing there looking at me laughing. I asked him why he stopped at the entrance and he told me that he was just wanted to keep me on my toes. When I lunged for him, he scampered away in hysterics. As we returned to the produce area, I saw a good friend and neighbor who was also picking up some produce items. She turned around, smiled and gave me a big hug when I tapped her on the shoulder. Jonathan stood there looking up at us when I introduced him to my neighbor. "Jonathan, this is Ms. Bonnie. Bonnie, this is Jonathan." Without hesitation he looked at her then at me and said, "She is not your wife. Is this your girlfriend?"

On our way back to the office I had to make one more stop: Office Depot. This time I made Jonathan go in ahead of me. But I should have known what he'd do-vanish in the huge space. He was having the time of his life making me look for him. Then I got wise to him and stopped looking for him. I just went about my business inspecting the flash drive and cover stock that I'd gone in for. Eventually Jonathan realized that I was not playing his game so he came back around to where I was shopping. Before long he was engrossed in some games that were on display. People noticed that we were together, many smiling as the two of us continued inspecting certain items. After a few minutes Jonathan came over to me with a game in his hand and before he could say a word, I said, "No!" Without a sound he turned, walked to the end of the aisle where the games were displayed and far enough away from me that I couldn't grab him. He turned around, holding the game above his head as he furthered himself from me and shouted down the isle at the top of his voice: "But DAD, you PROMISED!!!!"

The Demon Twins

The Summers family lived at 1510 Massachusetts Street, the north end of the block in a front basement apartment. The two youngest Summers brothers were twins: Melvin (Rabbit) and Alvin (Genie). They were young, strong, scary little black terrorists. If they wanted something, they took it, sometimes even from each other. They were not the type you spent time debating with. The reality was simple: they were predators and the rest of the kids on the block were prey. I was a just a snack, but I lived in fear. The twins devoted their waking hours to the dark side of life, the task of making every other kid's life miserable. They stalked; we fled. Luckily for me, they usually threatened and intimidated the bigger kids, those who offered some resistance. I offered no resistance. I was small fry and usually not big enough to bother with. That was little solace for me whenever I saw either of them coming toward me on the street. I had seen them both in action. So, I maintained a real low profile. In my mind the twins were life's way of telling me that the 'boogie man' was not only alive and well, but that he had a twin brother and they lived on my block. Though they lived down the block only a few houses from me, they lived in a totally different world than the other kids on the block.

"Rabbit" and "Genie" were the scourge of every kid on our block and a few nearby blocks. They were not identical twins and in fact, it was difficult to see how they might have been twins at all. Melvin, who was known as "Rabbit", the bigger and 'older' of the two, was built like a gladiator even though he was about my age. Even as a youngster, he had the body of a man; his black muscles were well defined, and his actions made it clear that he was as strong as he looked. He took every opportunity to let other kids on the block know just that. He stood tall and erect with thick lips and a wide nose and skin as black and rich as crude. There was no doubt he took pride in his physique since he often could be seen stalking around the neighborhood, bare chest and bare foot, his huge feet slapping against the pavement as he closed in on some hapless victim. He had hands like vices whose only real purpose was to inflict pain and suffering upon those who were unfortunate enough to fall into their grasps. His hair was short, thick, nappy and always uncombed; briar patch often came to mind. It stayed matted to his big head, a head that housed a brain with the IQ of a potato. It was doubtful that "Rabbit" could read or write; he stopped going to school when he was old enough to steal and he started stealing when he was old enough to walk. He was not my major concern. However, his twin brother, Alvin, known as "Genie", was shorter but nevertheless had a remarkably similar physique. He too was built strong with a set of muscles that indicated he was no physical weakling. Together they had inherited a code of behavior that set them apart from every other kid in the neighborhood. And as different as they were, in some ways, they were unquestionably related. Both were left-handed, both had admirable physiques and neither seemed to have had much mental aptitude. They thrived on what could only be called 'animal instincts'. But what made "Genie" look distinctly different from his twin sibling was that he was built low to the ground. He tended to slump forward when he stood or when he ran. And like a wolf, usually bare chest, he had a distinctly animal-like appearance that perfectly complimented his intellect. He was about my height, but much stronger. Looking back, I think now how he reminded me of the character in *Altered States* who, after some experimentation, was transformed to his original primal state, that state where man's natural predatory instincts were dominant. To me "Genie" was that guy. He was the closest thing I knew to a cave man who ate mayo and sugar sandwiches.

On one unfortunate occasion, when I got caught by this predator, he squeezed my arm so hard that I thought I would never use it again. His grip was a vice. My weapon was my mind. He was a real wild child. What really made him scary was that you never knew what he would do next. He was completely unpredictable. And his nose constantly ran. He'd just wipe most of the drippings away with the back of one of his ashy forearms, inhale the rest and keep going. I thought of him as the shorter half of the 'Snot Squad'. I was small in stature but that was no reason not to think like a giant. There was no way I could beat him up, but I could quietly call him all kinds of dirty names, the kind of names that he wouldn't understand even he heard them. Like his bigger sibling, his hair was a thick, matted, mass of steel wool. There was always something stuck in his hair. Things got stuck in his hair like a magnet. And together, whatever they wanted, they took. I was afraid of him and I hated him in spite of what the church ladies had taught us in Sunday school. But the church ladies didn't have to deal with him. He was the 'Bully from Hell' and unlike his 'smarter' brother, Genie had the IQ of a baked potato. Even so, I often wondered about him, his life, his brother's life and his family. I wondered if he was as happy as I was, especially at Christmas time. I wondered.

KING, QUEENIE, AND GENIE

It gets better. Wherever Genie went, King followed. And wherever King went, Queenie followed; the three were inseparable. King was a huge, ugly orange/brown/gray colored male mongrel dog with thick matted hair, much like that of his master. He followed Genie everywhere. Whenever Genie sneaked into Mr. Butts' drug store trying to steal something, King sat outside motionless, unchained with his eyes focused on the door to the store, waiting for his master's return. He dared not enter the store. Genie always came out running like in a gangster's movie, Mr. Butts hot on his tail. Nobody knows where King, the big canine came from; he had been around for as long as any of the kids could remember. He was just a part of the neighborhood landscape. I can't remember a time when

King was not around. If you saw one of them, you saw the others. Queenie was even uglier than King. She was a scrawny, one-eyed bitch that followed King everywhere; she was his mate. But King ruled the animal kingdom on the block and therefore no harm ever came to Queenie. There was no question in anybody's mind about that. King was clearly top dog and he did whatever Genie ordered him to do. Queenie, on the other hand, always went along for the ride. There was some special kind of communication between the three of them that nobody else could fathom, not even the other Summers kids. It was as though the three of them could read each other's minds, what little collective minds they had. Sometimes all it took was a subtle movement of Genie's eyes that sent King into action. At other times, it was an unintelligible verbal command that King responded to. Either way, when given a command, the dog responded. King knew all the kids on the block so he was never a threat to any of us so we all considered him one of us but he was not the kind of dog that you would want to pet. As in war, the kids on the block and throughout the neighborhood were civilians and hence were off limits to King. It was a different story, however, for strange dogs or cats that strayed onto the block. Rats were especially good hunting. It was at these times that King showed his true predatory skills. I saw how vicious he could be on command. Many dogs, cats and rats had perished in his huge jaws. Large or small, he simply took them in his jaws biting them and ferociously shaking the life out of them. Once lifeless, he would drop the limp carcass to the ground and sit at attention as if waiting for more orders from his master. The threesome feared only one person, Mr. Asbury Summers, the tall, dark, frail patriarch of the Summers clan.

The entry way to the Summers' apartment was in the front of the building, under the Galloways' concrete stairs. You'd have to go down a steep flight of crooked, brick steps that spiraled into a dark, dank cave-like area at the bottom, directly underneath. A single light bulb usually dangled from a frazzled overhead light fixture, creating creepy, moving shadows as it swung this way and that in the small space. It was creepy even during the daylight hours. The few times I went down those stairs, I was always with someone and never at night. Whenever I thought about Christmas, I wondered how Santa would negotiate those steep stairs at night in the snow and ice with a big heavy bag of toys on his back. What was worse, King lay at the bottom of the stairs at night, guarding his castle. He was like a big, ugly dragon, hiding down there in the dark, waiting to eat you.

I often wondered why the twins were so bad and why they lived in such a sad, dark place. I wondered if they had made that place sad by the way they acted or had that place made them act the way they did? I would have been sad, too if I had had to live in such a dark place like that with so many brothers and sisters who were always fighting with one another. I knew what it was like just to quarrel with Jo, my one sister and there were just the two of us. Being afraid of the dark didn't help me much either. The twins were bad boys, so I assumed they were getting punished. I was a good boy. I didn't hurt people and I didn't like to fight. My friends and I did not fight. We never even talked about fighting. That was because I couldn't fight. Sometimes Jo and I got into it, but she was my sister, and she was a girl and she always won.

It seemed that where we lived was the perfect metaphor for our lives. The Summers' home was a dark, gloomy place, below ground in 'Hell'. From their living room, you couldn't even look outside and see the sun. The sun would have to be nearly over head before the light could even penetrate their space. Their apartment was about eight feet below the sidewalk level. An area about six feet wide and the width of the building separated the front window from the wall supporting the sidewalk. It created a pit. From above at sidewalk level, you could look over the twisted wrought iron railing and down into the pit. There were two crooked railings that ran down length of the concrete stairs. It was a hazardous journey down those stairs, especially for someone as small as I was. The pit was usually filled with all kinds of junk; their front window faced a blank wall outside. It was a dark world they lived in and I felt so lucky that I lived second floor front, facing the light of the sun, in 'Heaven'.

Jonathan Kim

Episode 7: Fruit Loops

The one thing that Jonathan hated talking about more than anything was girls. He hated girls so I did all I could to keep the topics on girls. He bristled at every mention of the opposite sex. We began to have conversations about what he did and didn't like about them. Asked why he didn't like girls, he replied, "Girls have cooties!" Surprised at his answer, I asked him to repeat it. And he blurted out again, "Girls have cooties"! I asked where he got that idea. He simply reported, "My mom told me!" When I asked him if he knew what 'cooties' were, he said, "No, but girls got 'em". As our conversation continued, I tried to explain to him that sometimes girls seem to get in the way and are not cool. I assured him I knew because I had a sister. I assured him that as sure as sunrise, one day he was going to be thinking about nothing but girls. The stories I told him about my sister and me calmed him down a little but overall, according to him, if you didn't have a sister, girls were out. I predicted that one day if he didn't fall in love with a girl, a girl would fall in love with him and she would be so beautiful that it would difficult for him to ignore her.

When I asked him what he would do if that happened, he had no answer. And as if the cosmos looked upon me with a smile, the magic began. It was if I had written a script and the universe responded. Having learned from the past, I remembered to bring my camera along-much to Jonathan's dismay. He didn't like me taking his picture. He thought I was being childish whenever I took my camera out and began shooting.

We were at Salonica's, our favorite hangout. Jonathan looked handsome sitting across from me enjoying his favorite cereal, Fruit Loops. His bold black and yellow broad stripped polo shirt made him resemble a big, adorable bumble bee and I told him so. Just then a head popped up behind Jonathan in the next booth. It was a beautiful little girl who was standing on the seat in her booth. She looked to be East Indian. She was about Jonathan's age. She had the complexion of mocha with long, black shiny hair. She was truly a beautiful little girl. Our eyes met and I gave her a big smile as she stood taller on her side of the booth just behind Jonathan. She obviously had seen us when we first came in and took our seats. She immediately locked onto Jonathan. She wanted Jonathan and there was no doubt about it. But he was oblivious to what was happening. He had no idea she was only a few inches behind him. So, I let him know that I thought that today was the day a beautiful girl was going to fall in love with him. He scowled at me and continued eating his Fruit Loops. I said, "Jonathan, there's a very beautiful little girl standing behind you in the next booth and I think she's in love with you." He scowled again, ignoring my warning. So, I dared him. "Ok, if you don't believe, me I dare you to turn around." He ignored me again, so I said, "I Double Dare you to turn around." No response. Applying pressure I said, "I Double Dog Dare you to turn around." He accepted the DDD, swiveled on his seat and to his utter shock, found himself face to face, inches away from the little girl's face. Jonathan screamed aloud from the shock. I laughed along with other patrons in the restaurant. He looked incredulous and refused to turn around again. I couldn't stop laughing as I continued taking pictures. I said, "Jonathan she's coming around to our booth!" His unintentional scream had gotten the attention of other customers, so they began tuning into the budding romance occurring right in front of them. Before I could say another word, the little girl had left her booth, come around and jumped up on Jonathan's seat, looking at him and smiling at him from ear to ear. For a long moment she just sat there, staring into his eyes with a look of infatuation that was undeniable. I couldn't believe it. I just continued taking pictures. Every time she scooted closer to Jonathan, he scooted backward until his back was against the wall. She continued to come closer until they were touching. Jonathan was trapped. The look on his face said, "This is not happening." But it was happening, and I had gotten photos of the entire episode. I considered it good blackmail material. Together they looked like the perfect picture of interracial harmony. Then I realized that not only was she wearing a pink sweater, but it was emblazoned with dozens of tiny pink hearts. Customers at other tables began applauding the little melodrama. Jonathan sat there speechless, in total shock. The little girl sat there close to him, smiling, looking up right into his eyes. After a few minutes a woman in the next booth came to our booth and apologized for the intrusion and said that her daughter, Saronia, had never done anything like that before. I assured her that there was absolutely no need for apologies; and that Saronia was welcome to stay if she liked. Saronia had made my day. The woman confessed that her daughter was clearly smitten with Jonathan as soon as she saw us come into the restaurant and sit in the next booth. The mother and I were both amazed and amused at how determined Saronia was to meet Jonathan. It was a true 'love at first sight' event and we both laughed as the two of them sat staring into each other's eyes, Saronia in heaven and Jonathan backed against the wall in hell. When I told him that I couldn't' wait to tell his mother about the incident, Jonathan pleaded with me to keep it a secret. So, from that day forward, any time Jonathan decided he would give me grief, I would threaten to show Seon and anybody and everybody in the bank the photos of him and Saronia. That threat always calmed him down, but it was a short-lived advantage I held because soon he completely ignored my thin threats. I showed the photo to his mother, his father and anybody who would look at them. Without exception, everyone who saw them were touched. After that incident, whenever the topic of girls came up, Jonathan refused to talk; instead he would just roll his eyes at me. That always brought me a big laugh. *Touché,* Denver.

Can You See Me Now?

In 1988 we bought our first condominium. It was in Hyde Park, located on the southeast corner of 51st Street at Cornell Ave. We were one flight up. The apartment was unique. Though it was a three bedroom, two bath unit, it was laid out in a very interesting way. When you entered, to the right was the living room, with a door leading to the balcony and a door leading to the bedroom next to it. That bedroom also had a door leading out to the balcony. Adjoining this bedroom was a full bath. And adjoining the full bath was the main bedroom. Completing the circular tour, a door leaving the bedroom led out to the hall. Looking backward down the hall was where we entered the apartment. At this juncture, we're standing at the dining room. This point is the half-way point of the apartment. From this point on, it's in a straight line. Past the dining room was the kitchen and beyond that was the third bedroom which I converted to my space. The apartment had some unique features: a wall safe in the front bedroom off the balcony and it had a floor-installed bell ringer, under the dining room table which would allow the owners to summon the cook while having dinner. The building was constructed sometime in the late 1800's and was obviously built for those with wealth. At that time, 51st Street in Hyde Park was considered the outskirts of Chicago when heading south. Wealthy white people owned all the property constructed in those days. This was before there were even sidewalks in the area. The entire area was new construction. Sand dunes surrounded the entire structure; the "neighborhood" was non-existent.

I tried to imagine what it would have been like to have looked over my balcony to the street just below and see nothing but sand. And having a corner apartment gave us access to both 51ˢ St and 51st & Cornell Ave. The building went from 51st & Cornell Ave. over to and around 51st & Hyde Park Blvd. It was a big building, and every apartment had a balcony. Those with the best view were the owners on the third floor whether on the Cornell Ave. side or the busy 51st Street side. Balconies were the redeeming grace of the building and every owner cherished them. During the summer months we spent most of the warm evenings sitting on the balcony watching passersby walking their dogs, U of Chicago students running to catch their campus buses and passengers disembarking from the 51st Street bus that stopped right below our balcony. We sat just above the pedestrian traffic below us, just high enough that hardly anyone knew we were there. Often our neighbor, Bonnie would pass by and look up, acknowledging the fact that we were usually enjoying the summer warmth. Likewise, we could often find Bonnie sitting on her balcony which was one door down on the same level as ours. A few of our good neighbor friends lived higher up on the third floor, eliminating our ability to see them unless they came to the edge of their perches and looked over.

In 2003 after fifteen years in the condo, my wife, Joan and I bought a house further south and miles away from our friends in the condo building. We both missed seeing our old neighbors and would often call them on the phone just to say hello. Whenever I rode my bike to Hyde Park on the bike path, I would ride by the apartment building, get my phone out and call one of my neighbors. Often, they'd respond by coming out on the balcony to greet me. Minutes would go by as we chatted and got reacquainted. Sometimes a neighbor would come down with their bike and together we'd ride along the bike path. My wife never rode her bike to Hyde Park but whenever she was in the area, she'd call one of them and be greeted with happy cheers. Our neighbors were always happy to hear from us especially when we came to Hyde Park in person and took the time to reach out and hello.

The years passed but the customary phone calls from the street to the balconies of our old neighbors continued whenever either of us was in the 51st St area. One day Joan, was in Hyde Park and decided to walk over to the building to say hello to one of our friends in the building. Ken lived on the third floor and was always happy to look down and greet either of us. "Hello, Ken. It's Joan. I'm in your neighborhood and downstairs under your balcony," she said into the phone. Excited, Ken said, "Oh, great. It'll be good to see you again. Give me a minute and I'll be on the balcony." After about five minutes Ken said, "Joan, where are you? I don't see you. "I'm standing under your balcony, but I don't see you, either. I'm on the Cornell Avenue side of the building. Can you see me now? I'm looking up at your balcony," Joan explained. Ken began laughing uncontrollably. He explained that he was indeed standing on his third-floor balcony, looking down for Joan. The problem was Joan was looking up in Chicago. Ken was looking down from his balcony in Tampa.

Little White Corvette

It was during a visit to Freetown, as a few of us volunteers were walking around the city, that I saw what I thought could only have been a hallucination. It happened so fast that I couldn't be sure. Several others in the group said they had seen it, too. A few minutes later our suspensions were confirmed. Coming down the street right in front of us was an African American man, driving a brand new white, convertible 1967 Chevy Corvette. A white Corvette on the road in Freetown, Sierra Leone didn't seem real. Not long after seeing the car, I met its owner. His name was Lou, a brother from Minnesota. He was a contract employee, like Peace Corps except that he got paid, a lot. His company shipped his 'Vette' to Freetown. He was also in town for the big party being thrown by one of the Peace Corps officials who lived and worked in the city. Lou was a true Renaissance man, immediately likeable. He had all the attributes most guys would kill for. With all that going for him he was still a humble, modest guy. The proverbial, 'tall, dark and handsome' guy, Lou was funny, too. He looked like an athlete. He could sing. He could play the guitar. He could play the piano. He could even dance, a little, truly a brilliant guy, he could make you laugh. His trouble was getting the girl. I figured if Lou couldn't get a girl, there was something wrong. He was not gay; and he lusted just like the rest of us. He was just Lou. We bonded immediately. Lou was the envy of every guy at the party. All the guys wanted to be him. Yet oddly enough, of all people there, Lou admired me. I even learned how to use a darkroom in Lou's second bedroom at his house in Makena. He taught me how to develop film. Guitar lessons also came with the friendship. He said I had an easy way with the girls that came naturally but he had to work at it. There were so many girls that it was hard to keep up.

My main objective was to say something to Kuniashi Segura whom everybody called "Kuni". She was Japanese, twenty-one years old and one of only three Asian volunteers in the entire program at the time. So just by numbers alone, she was not only desirable but rare. Kuni was a photographer back home in San Francesco and she always had a camera with her. But because of the high-spirited party and all the hyper-activity, the time got by me, and I missed my opportunity to approach her. It wasn't like other girls escaped my attention. So many choices. So little time. But Kuni was my fantasy, my big fantasy. She was the one all the guys wanted to boink. Any dude lucky enough to hook up with Kuniashi Segura deserved it. We had met before early in our tour when we first got in the country. She was impressed with the fact that I attended the School of the Art Institute of Chicago. Kuni was of the 'anything Chicago' school. It was the music scene she loved, the jazz scene. I was surprised. She especially loved anything having to do with The Art Institute of Chicago and its renowned art school. For the moment, all I could do was fantasize; it always helped in the past and it didn't cost anything. The party was a blast as it went on into the night. And then it was over. But because of the high-spirited atmosphere and the hyper-activity, the time got by me, and I missed my opportunity to approach Kuni. I kicked myself.

Partiers assembled outside and began to leave, dispersing into the night. Suddenly from the side of the residence roared an engine. It was the little white Corvette. There was Lou, revving the engine loudly and tearing away from the premises. He was having his moment. The smile on his face said everything. He was the true victor of the night. Sitting next to him with her hair blowing back in the wind was Kuniashi 'Kuni' Segura. This was Lou's get even scene, like in the movies when the good guy gets the girl in the end. This was the scene in the movie where they drive off into the sunset with victory music blaring in the background. Most guys would have given a lot for that very 'fifteen minutes of Lou's fame.' I was very impressed. I went home alone.

I couldn't wait to see Lou so that he could give me the lowdown on Kuni. I knew he would have lots to talk about, even boast about if he saw fit. I was feeling a bit jealous but still happy for Lou who had made some serious progress with his efforts. When I was finally able to catch him and question him about Kuni, he seemed a bit reluctant to talk about it. I pressed him. After much insistence, he finally relented. He said his hopes were high when he left the party with Kuni. They laughed a lot at first. She started talking about photography. Lou could hold his own when it came to photography. He even had his own darkroom. He was doing good; he might even get lucky as he had hoped. Her plan was to travel the world taking pictures when her tour in Sierra Leone was over. She and a few other young women in county had made their plans early on and admitted that their journey would probably last two years if they did everything they had planned. Lou related how he could feel the strong determination in Kuni's character. He let her do all the talking. In that way the less he said, the less he could screw up. Looking good. Then, to Lou's surprise, Kuni asked, "Didn't Denver go to the SAIC?" "Yeah, I think he did", Lou responded. He could immediately feel the conversation going in the wrong direction. Then he said that they were together for just about one hour then he took her home. "Why"? I asked. Sheepishly, he said that for the rest of the evening, all Kuni was interested in was Denver Long. Finally, he promised her that he'd introduce us. Initially I thought Lou was kidding me just to get a laugh. But the look on his face said it all, again. Kuni Segura wanted to hang with me! I was shocked.

Kuni and I met a day later. Without effort we were together for the next two days. The evening before we all had to leave Freetown and head back up country, Kuni and spent on the beach. We had blankets, smoking materials, matches and something 'special' that Kuni brought for the occasion. High life music played softly off in the distance, we kept our short-wave radios on hand just in case. The BBC was always an option. Our blankets were spread out onto the warm sand. Together we watched, amazed, at the beauty of the sun slowly melting into the magnificent Atlantic Ocean. Our fumbling inability to get a fire going right away made the whole experience so memorable, romantic, and funny. It took a while before a fire came to life, but once we got it going, it roared. Behind us and looming ominously over our heads, for the length of the dark beach in either direction were huge jagged boulders, disappearing into the darkness. We camped underneath them. It was our beach; it was our memorable moment, or at least it was for me. We lay there in silence as I recalled painting this picture in my mind when I was a kid. Without thinking, I said, "Kuni, you didn't know this, but I actually met you when I was about twelve years old, back in Gary, Indiana." "What are you talking about?", she laughed out loud. "Kuni, when I was a kid, I used to spend a lot of my time alone, in my room dreaming about all of the things that I would do when I grew up. I was a super-nerd. I wondered why Santa Claus and Jesus Christ weren't running buddies. Everybody thought I was weird. I was. But I understood something inside, about the nature of life that nobody else seemed to understand or even be aware of. I wasn't into sports; I was into books and the mind. I was searching for the answer to life. I used to dream about traveling to foreign countries and meeting beautiful girls. I dreamed of falling in love in exotic foreign lands, always with a beautiful girl. You were one of them or you wouldn't be here. I was in love with you when I was twelve and you about nine. I didn't know your name then but I knew we'd meet one day in a foreign land." Kuni said nothing. I continued: "At this moment, Kuni, you are the most beautiful creature in the universe to me. I say this because you were there in my dream, when I was a child, when I needed something to look forward to. It was you." Jokingly I continued: "Of course I dreamed of and fantasized about a lot of girls, you know? But Kuni, there is only one time. It is not the past; that's gone. It's not the future; that's not here yet. The only time is now. And right now, at this very moment, I am living in a reality that just yesterday was a dream. With you!" Without intent, I had given her the most heartfelt love story I could have imagined. I felt so in love at that moment that I almost made myself cry. Instead, Kuni started to tear. "I have never, ever had anyone say such things to me before. Who are you? No one has ever told me that they met me when they were twelve and I was a kid! Denver, I am so moved that I don't know what to say. "Say, yes," I whispered. We laughed for a long time.

She was not only beautiful, but she was very exotic. It was the most romantic night of my entire life. Kuni said she felt the same way and that there was no denying that the environment and setting were special. She looked like a model, the kind of girl that any guy would say "yes" to but be too reluctant to approach. Her hair was pitch black and shiny; it reached her waist when let out. Most of the time she kept it rolled up tight so that you'd never know its real length. It was also much easier to keep clean. To my surprise, she wanted to know more about me than I had expected. Her interests in me seemed genuine and I felt flattered and a little embarrassed. However, my thoughts at that moment were not so noble; I was thinking more about no bra and wet panties. Segura was a little taller than me, but it didn't seem to matter. I was taken by her stunning body and tried hard not to be too obvious about my staring. Though she wore shorts and a thin top, I could tell she was very comfortable with me seeing that there was indeed no bra underneath her flimsy shirt. Her breasts acknowledged me as I attempted to remain calm and in control. I was not in complete control.

Suddenly Kuni jumped up as she remembered what she had put in her bag that was 'special' for us. She reached into her bag and took out a smaller canvas bag containing something wrapped carefully in tissue. My curiosity was peaked, and she reached into the bag again and slowly brought out a bottle. It was a bottle of sake, Japanese rice wine. The tissue protected two small porcelain cups. "Have you ever had sake?" she asked. "No", I responded. As I watched, Kuni leveled a little sand near the fire and sat the bottle of sake near the fire. "It's best when it's warm; we'll give it a few minutes to warm up", she explained. I suddenly remembered what I had brought 'special' for us, too. I reached into my knapsack and took a small package carefully wrapped. I had one joint and I lit it. We smoked and sipped sake. After about an hour, we were in a state of bliss. The ganja was incredible, and the sake sent me sailing like I've never sailed before. Sake is 'sneaky'. It's like you're sipping warm, weak wine and then you're drunk.

There was something impressive about the way Kuni carried herself; it was not arrogance but confidence. Without prompting, she admitted openly to me that she was aware of how most of the guys in the group just wanted to have sex with her. Without warning, I asked, "Ever been

with a black guy?" For the first time I saw her blush. "No",
she responded with a sheepish smile that surprised me.
Looking into each other's eyes, we both laughed excitedly.
"I've never been with a Japanese girl either." We laughed
again, this time with less frivolity. The music, ganja, and
sake were working together to ignite the atmosphere; it
was electric when, to my total astonishment and delight,
she asked, "Do you want to make love with me here on the
beach?"

Gabby

In 1995 I became the first Director of the Upward Bound Program at Robert Morris College in Chicago. The program, which is adopted by many colleges and universities is federally funded and provides training for inner city high school students who want to attend college. The program required that the selected students maintain a certain grade level in their respective schools, and attend required classes located on the respective campuses on the weekends. The main purpose of the program was to give high school students the experience of living on a campus, attending classes, and developing good study habits that they would need in college. The students are given a weekly stipend that covers their travel expenses to and from program activities and other necessities. The program lasts for three years during which time the students focus on preparing themselves for college; the institution also assists the students in preparing for admissions testing and all other priorities related to college life. Staff members are focused on helping the students maintain their focus on attending college. As Director of the program, it was my responsibility to locate a college that provided campus living since Robert Morris

College did not have a campus. Once a college agreed to take part in the program, Upward Bound students moved into the dorms and attended classes like regular college students. Students were also encouraged to apply for a passport. When they completed their passport applications, the program paid the fees. Finally, once in the three-year period, the students are taken on a trip which meant flying on an airplane, something very few of the students had ever done. Of the fifty students in the program, thirty-five were girls and fifteen to sixteen were boys, all between the ages of fifteen and seventeen years. A major part of getting the program started was recruiting the students to fill the openings. My job meant that I would have visit selected schools that my program was designed to service and interview them. The process was both exciting and exhausting. Once the word spread that a college recruiter was visiting schools to interview kids for a special program, the pool of eligible students grew greatly. The boys were given seminars on proper behavior to exhibit in public, how to dress properly when out and how to show respect to young women, whether they were in the program or not. The girls were advised by their female teachers, on how to dress properly in public and other subjects pertinent to their growth. On one occasion per year, the students and staff go out to dinner at a pre-selected restaurant. The students are taught proper table manners, how to use the cutlery and other social skills. Most of the students were either African American or Hispanic; the Asian students came in third. The teaching staff was reflective of the student body, one teacher from each of the student ethnic groups. All women, they represented the diversity of the student body and provided the much-needed closeness that some of the young women in the program sought.

One such young woman who entered the program after its second year was Gabiola, a junior in high school and a straight A student. She was a very quiet, very reserved little Hispanic girl. If you didn't see her, you wouldn't know she was in the room. With soft blonde hair, she kept to herself and spoke in near whispers whenever she was called on. Having met her mother during the interview process, I could see right away where she got her shyness. I had made it clear to the students at the beginning of the program that if they ever had any problems that they needed to discuss, I my door would always be open. Many students took advantage of the opportunity to bare their souls to me in private conversations. After hearing the personal problems that many were having at home and at school, it was easy to understand why some performed the way they did. For too many, their problems prevented them from seeing beyond their present circumstances. Living in another city or going to a college away from home just seemed impossible to most of them. Some had never even been to downtown Chicago. The staff and I worked diligently to change that and to show the students that they could accomplish anything that they set their minds to. The important thing was to have the courage to dream and go for it. I was determined to help in any way I could. My budget was specifically designated for the assistance of the students.

Gabiola, whom all the students called Gabby, was different in many ways from the other students. And though she was almost invisible, she had a dream and she shared it with me one morning when we met in the hall and she asked if we could talk in private. Once we were alone in the classroom, she told me about her dream in a voice so soft that I had to keep asking her to repeat parts of it. She did not want to share her dream with the other students for fear of being ridiculed and laughed at. Gabby confessed to me that she wanted to go to France. I was surprised and delighted. I gave her a big hug and she responded with the biggest smile I had ever seen from her. I told her that I would do everything I could to encourage her and to make sure she accomplished her dream. From that conversation on, Gabby was a different person. She had a light in her eyes that I had never seen before and she began smiling more. I shared with her that like in my childhood, I remembered how much I lived in my mind, putting all the details into my dream and making sure that I constantly nurtured it with pictures and books and music and anything that would keep the dream alive in my head. I shared my personal story with Gabby and from that exchange we grew close. My advice was to "Become French." Learn as much as she could about France: learn the language, the food, the people, the cities, and customs, learn everything

It wasn't long before I saw clear and unquestionable evidence that my advice was being heeded. In addition to her uniform which was always immaculate and neat, Gabby began wearing white knee-high socks that stopped just short of the bend in her legs. She began wearing a matching white beret. Her beret and knee socks soon became her trademark. And to my utter astonishment, whenever Gabby approached me and spoke, she would take out a little black French translation book. Gabby was learning French. Before she said anything she would open the book and attempt to say it in French. I was totally impressed. Slowly the other students became more inquisitive and realized that Gabby was very serious in her transformation. Her entire personality began to sparkle; she began to talk more openly to the other students. Smiles became her new calling card. When my superiors heard about it, they gave me and the program high praise for the obvious benefits it was providing the students. I had high hopes for my students.

In my mind's eye, I was the student in the Upward Bound Program, dreaming about my future and how I was going to get to Italy. From my past life experience, it seemed easy to get to France, but I could just imagine what Gabby was going through. And what I had learned from childhood was that when you begin to live in your dream is when it becomes real. Like me, Gabby was strolling the streets of Paris in her mind, enjoying the sights as she laughed and joked with her French friends. I was Gabby; Gabby was me. Living a dream meant that the environment must respond to you in that very same way. With Gabby I would do all that I could to encourage her to 'live' in France every day; she was becoming a little blonde French girl right before our eyes.

One Saturday morning Gabby and I talked about college. Asked where she wanted to attend college, she didn't know. In fact, she questioned the whole idea of being able to go to college. She was shocked in disbelief when I suggested she apply to a college in France; there was absolutely nothing she had to lose. Though stunned, she agreed and together with my help and her mother's devoted efforts and insistence, she began completing dozens and dozens of forms and applications and more forms. I paid the fees associated with applying. As if by destiny, my prior decision to require students to apply for a U.S passport was perfectly timed. So, in addition to the dozens of pages of documents she had to complete, Gabby was also applying for her first U.S. passport. Upward Bound was changing lives for the good.

The program grew and became a beacon of RMC's enlightened environment for high school students. By now I had been moved from my basement location up to the fourth floor to a real office. I had my own computer, telephone, desk, and I even had a window. The program was doing wonderfully; grades were improving, parents were happy, my boss was happy and again I was living in a dream. So, to demonstrate our progress and growth, I decided to take the students on a trip, a trip to our nation's capital, Washington, D.C. When word got out that the program was taking the kids on a plane to Washington, D. C., attendance improved dramatically, attitudes changed for the better, conversations became polite, and an undercurrent of excitement permeated the program. Not one of the students had ever been on a plane. Planning for the trip demanded my full attention. There were so many details to attend to and time suddenly seemed to speed up the closer we got to departure day. Three of the female teachers were going on the trip along with me and about forty-five students. I sought out advice from other directors about which hotels to consider and what agendas to prepare once we landed in the capital. Most of the students going on the trip were young women whose grades far exceeded those of the boys. My primary concern was for the safety and protection of every student. With that in mind, I referred to my much earlier training as a Young Men's Division member in NSA, later becoming SGI (Soka Gakkai International).

As a Young Men's Division member in NSA it was always important to maintain harmony and to work together in unison with those participating. The goal was to promote unity that reflects the principle of many in body one in mind (*itai doshin*). The safety and protection of every individual member was the foremost concern whenever the organization went on a 'movement' to promote world peace. Working together to protect one another was the outstanding hallmark of the organization's youth divisions. In the case of Robert Morris College and Upward Bound, traveling across the country as a group required the same kind of attention paid to safety and protection. So, I held regular meetings with all of the young men in the Upward Bound Program, emphasizing the importance of them respecting and protecting the young women in the program. For the boys to learn to accept the responsibility of protecting their classmates as brothers and sisters was a big step forward in the building of their characters; they chose readily to welcome the opportunity to show their maturity. It was just as important for the girls to act accordingly when traveling with the group, too. The women teachers were there at every turn to assure that proper conduct was always adhered to.

By the time the trip rolled around, we were ready and well prepared. Hotel reservations had been secured with the students having chosen their own roommates. Flights had been arranged for the group; sightseeing agendas had been completed. And to top it all, when we departed, we were all attired in our 'traveling whites' uniforms. Everybody in the group was wearing white jeans with matching white shirts emblazoned with the RMC Upward Bound logo and matching white caps. It was truly a multi-racial group, and I was so proud to be its director. In our preparatory meetings it was decided that since most of the group were girls, then there would be two boys assigned to each group, along with one teacher. The boys were to act as chaperones and the girls were expected to cooperate. When traveling around the capital, no one was to ever travel alone. And if anyone broke the rules and conducted themselves in an improper manner, I assured them that, with or without their parents' consent. I would immediately have them arrested and executed. The students and teachers laughed at that but they all knew that I was very serious. Any disobedience on the trip and that student would be terminated from the program when we returned.

At the airport students wandered around in their respective groups waiting for our flight to be called. Many strangers approached us, asking who this well-mannered diverse student body was. When told that we were Robert Morris College's Upward Bound students bound for Washington, D.C., they were very impressed. People were taking our pictures, talking to the students, and asking questions about the Upward Bound program.

I was chanting softly for most of the day as we waited to board our plane. Then our flight was called, and students began jumping up and down, the girls hugging one another. Each student marched onto the plane as though they were receiving an academy award. I felt overwhelming pride in what we were about to do. Once everyone was seated and settled on the plane, I could almost hear the rapid heartbeats from the rear of the cabin as I strode down the aisle making sure everyone was on board. Eyes were wide, nervous conversations shot back and forth across the aisle, from row to row at breathtaking speeds. Excitement and fear both filled the enclosed space. From time to time, I looked back into the plane to make sure everybody was ok. Suddenly we were moving backward, away from the ramp and for a moment all talking stopped. Eyes scanned the small windows as they darted around the cabin to see how fellow students were coping. As the plane roared down the runway, hearts raced; there wasn't a sound in the cabin. I looked back into the cabin and laughed as some of the students' faces strained to reflect the fear as hands grasped armrests with desperation. Many knuckles turned white. I think many of the students reaffirmed their faith in God as the plane soared higher and higher. Once the plane leveled off, little changed. The students were taken aback by the sensation of being motionless. There were still some white knuckles. I laughed halfway to the capital. But by the time the plane landed at National International Airport in D.C., I was among a bunch of pros. When our bus pulled up in front of our D.C. hotel, the young men on the bus, knowing what to do, jumped off the bus first, before the girls. They quickly off loaded the luggage so that by the time the last girl and teachers had exited the bus, all bags were lined up along the curb, ready for pick up. The hotel had been notified of our scheduled arrival and was ready for us. Once all the students had entered the hotel and proceeded to their rooms, the hotel manager approached me and said that he had never, ever seen such a large, well behaved, polite, and diverse, group of kids. I gave him a list of every student in the group and how their families could be notified in case of some dire emergency. We talked about all the tourists in Washington and the tremendous number of students that travel to the capital every year. Over the years, the manager had seen hundreds of thousands of students. His hotel catered to colleges and high schools. In our conversations about education, he asked me what my discipline philosophy was. I said, "Immediate arrest and execution." We both laughed.

Up to this point, nothing more could have been asked of the students. They were magnificent. The planned agenda indicated that at this point, everyone, once settled into their rooms would gather for lunch in the hotel dining room and then go out for an afternoon of sightseeing. A set time was agreed upon to meet back at the hotel at the end of the day. We divided up into four groups of about eleven students with one instructor and at least two boys per group. I took the fourth group and then we all went our separate ways. Back at the hotel that first night, after everyone had eaten dinner, the students started partying. Our Upward Bound group had nearly the entire floor to ourselves so that we wouldn't cause any disturbances to the other occupants of the hotel. But there had been no need for concern. Every room occupied by the students had its door open so that there was a constant flow of visitors from one room to the next. There was music and dancing and laughter that started the moment we arrived back at the hotel. From my room, I could hear the celebrations going on down the hall and around the corner, but they were surprisingly controlled considering the number of young people who were participating. Suddenly a group of students were knocking on my door begging me to come and dance. I agreed on condition they got the teachers to dance with us, so they did and the party went on. My time to leave the party came upon me so I thanked the students for such a good time. I reminded everybody, especially the boys, that there would be no roommate swapping, as we all laughed, and I said good night. The next few days of the trip were just as marvelous as the first day. Whenever we ended the day back at the hotel, the students exchanged stories about the museums they had visited and the monuments they had seen and even some politicians that some of them had seen. The trip to Washington was a complete and total success as every student in the group agreed.

The flight back to Chicago wasn't nearly as scary as the one was to D.C. By now the students were much more confident about themselves since they had come on the trip. When our bus finally pulled up in front of Robert Morris College late in the evening, the young men on the bus knew exactly what to do as they jumped into action, unloading the luggage, and lining it up along the sidewalk. All the waiting parents were truly impressed with the order, harmony, and joy that they saw in the students as they disembarked. We had all returned home safely having shared, for some, a four-day experience of a lifetime.

Weeks had passed since Gabby sent off her forms and applications for scholarships, admissions, tests, passport applications, photos and other required documents. A big part of her challenge was that her parents, especially her mother was not that well versed at reading and writing English, so Gabby relied much more on a relative and me to get all of her required paperwork completed. Then one Saturday morning Gabby came to class beaming with joy. Her passport had come in the mail the day before. She was so very proud that she passed it around the classroom so that everyone could see it. And in the photo, there was Gabby looking a bit nervous but donning her white beret and a timid half smile. Her accomplishment had only served to inspire the other students to hurry and get their passports too, because rumors of Gabby applying to colleges overseas had begun to spread around the campus. Then week by week she received one piece of good news after the other. First, she received word that she had passed her battery of tests that were required before she could seriously enroll in any college, whether foreign or domestic. Then, after having sent applications to a half dozen schools, she got two letters expressing interest in her coming to study in Paris. On this morning, Gabby showed up at school with her mother, each of them crying. I was immediately concerned about what she had been through. As I approached the two of them, Gabby spoke for her mother as she handed me a letter and a package. When we all thought that it couldn't get any better, it did. Gabby had won a scholarship to study abroad. I was caught off guard by the way the good news had been brought to me. I read the letter that said she had been granted funding to study in Paris for the term of one full year. In the other package was a brand-new necktie that her mother had bought for me to express her deep appreciation. Her mother reached out and hugged me, crying as she did. Then Gabby reached out and put her arms around the both of us, crying as she did. I reached out and embraced the two of them, crying as I did. So, there we were, the three of us, standing in the middle of the busy hall, hugging one another, and all of us crying like babies while students stared in disbelief as they walked around us heading for their classes. It was quite a scene.

Gabby went to France and lived for a year and what made the story even more amazing was the fact that before she left Paris, her mother was able to travel to France and visit her. How that happened is still a mystery to me. Gabby sent me a post card letting me know that her dream had come true and that had it not been for me and the Upward Bound Program at Robert Morris College, she would never have made it. By the time I moved on from Robert Morris College, three students had not only gotten passports but had traveled outside of the United States, one later permanently moving to Spain. I was living my life all over again vicariously through these students, knowing that the little spark inside that begins to burn brighter and hotter when nurtured, was truly within all of us. It only took something or someone to point it out.

Mary Laube

It has been fourteen years since Kay passed away in 2008 and over fifty-five years since we were a couple in college (1965). I think of her often. Those fun times in school passed so quickly. I often have vivid flashbacks of the those funny, exciting, and expansive years we shared. Not having seen Kay for decades, her passing away comes to me a bit less painfully. I still laugh when I recall the crazy things that we did and said to one another, not realizing how profoundly they would affect our futures. I think of the little girl (Mary) and her brother (Edward) who were in the photo Kay had sent me. It was funny because I identified little Mary in the photo as the "unmixed" kid she adopted. Kay and I had joked about race when we were in school, laughing about our "mixed" kids. My mind often takes me there and I find myself smiling, sometimes even laughing out loud. It was always a pleasant ride to the past.

One day in 2018 while I was on the internet, the name Mary Laube crossed my screen, but I ignored it. Then I saw that same name appear again on my Iphone's "Messenger app". Whoever this Mary was, I assumed she must know me because she was sending me a text message. I opened it and the text read:

"Dear Denver,

I hope this message finds you well. My name is Mary Laube. I am the daughter of Kay Laube (formerly known as Kay DiNovo). I am an artist/professor currently in Knoxville TN. I was doing some research on my mom's time at SAIC and came across your book Professor Buddha. I was amazed and moved by your story. Chapter 10 is the most detailed account I have of her, and I wanted you to know how meaningful this is to me. I remember a long, long time ago she told me about you, and it didn't occur to me until I was finished with the section on the DiNovo Sanction that you were the one in my mother's story. I understand the potential awkwardness of me contacting you out of the blue, but I wanted to ask if you would be interested in having a conversation sometime. Below is my contact information. Thank you again.

Warmly, Mary Laube."

I was dumbfounded! It was Kay's *'unmixed'* Korean adopted daughter who was in the photo Kay sent me in 1994. She must have been all of nine years old in the photo. She must be in her thirties now. Without hesitation I texted:

"Mary, I am dumbfounded! I am searching for words to say", I continued. That one photo was all that I knew of Mary Laube. I included my telephone number in my text. Mary said that she would be available for conversation shortly. I responded: "At your convenience". An hour later my phone rang. I was excited; it was Mary Laube. Our voices reflected our mutual excitement. She explained how she had miraculously come across my book _Professor Buddha_ with a story in it about her mother, Kay DiNovo. We shared the amazement.

Mary was married and had moved to Knoxville, TN about two years earlier to take an art professorship at a university. She was the mother of a son and was currently pregnant, expecting her second child in the months to come. I made it a point of predicting the gender of the new baby. I said emphatically, "It's a boy and I'm going to call him "Denden", I exclaimed. We both laughed at the idea. As I listened to her, she immediately reminded me of her mother and her mother's dedication to the arts and education. Without a doubt Kay would be as dumbfounded as I am to know that her daughter and I, her boyfriend from fifty years ago have somehow come together in the present. It is an incredible story. Months later Mary had her second child; it was a boy. I was surprised that both sons were born a few years apart in the month of May. When I first saw a picture of Mary and her two beautiful sons, it immediately brought back memories of the photo that Kay had sent me. I pointed out the irony of the 'heritage' that was being transferred from one generation to another. To complete the celebration of our relationship, I told Mary that I was 'adopting' her and her two sons. From one artist/professor to another, I welcomed her into my life as my "daughter". We laughed and saluted Kay for bringing us together. We agreed to be 'pen pals.' That idea made us both laugh. We agreed that letter writing was dead. I suggested to Mary that she inform the men in her life that they were now part of my family. Tell the hubby and the two boys, especially the youngest one, the one they nicknamed Denden.

Ma

It was Wednesday, October 19, 2016. My mother was on her death bed. I sat at her bedside. The doctors said that it was just a matter of time, maybe hours. Years earlier she had been diagnosed with Alzheimer's Disease. She'd been in a deep coma for the last month. Her condition had worsened over previous weeks. It had reached the point where she and I could no longer converse. However, that did not stop me from visiting regularly, holding her hand, and talking to her any way. The first thing I always did when I entered her softly lit room was to place my smart phone next to her head on the side table. Very softly, *Nam myoho renge kyo* played. The audio lasted for fifteen minutes then I'd play it over and over. I made sure it was playing whenever I left the room. The sound of the chanting created a very peaceful space. It had been about two years since my mother, and I had held any semblance of a real conversation. Growing up, we had held some intense and invigorating discussions and debates. When I was a kid, she was my mother, mentor, and debate coach. I could always bounce ideas off her and get valuable feedback. If we disagreed on something, most of the time we discussed it and came to some understanding. I learned the importance of listening and hearing what the other person was saying. I was taught that the most important part of the conversation was listening. She taught me not to listen just to respond but to listen with the intent of understanding. Often my mother challenged me unexpectedly and would say, "Spell exuberant" or "spell psychosis" or some word that she thought might trip me up. Or unexpectedly she'd say, "What does query mean?" Most of the time I got the spelling right and definition correct; then I'd throw another word back at her. She always did better than me. But those challenges kept me busy learning new words and meanings and how to spell. They kept my head in books where I was always comfortable. "What's the capitol of Vermont?" I was always ready for a word challenge.

Whenever I entered her room, I would lean over, and give mom a kiss on her forehead. The male nurse was there, sitting quietly in a corner of the room. The mood was not especially sad; my mother was not in any pain as she had been in the past. She was at home in her own bed. She would be happy to know that I was there, talking as I had always done in the past whether someone was listening or not. She took great parental pride in my brilliant silliness. In the past whenever I went to see her, I had made it my duty to make her laugh and lift her spirit-no matter what. The crazier my attempt, the better. It had always worked in the past. The funny thing was that most of the things I told my mother were true personal experiences. Over the many years growing up, I always admitted much of my mischief to her in a way that would make her shake her head and laugh. In that way I could always stay a step ahead of an ass whoopin' in case the facts came to light before my confessions. My mom and I always had a fantastic relationship. To make her laugh now was not in the offing but that did not dampen my enthusiasm in the least. She could sense my silliness. When I was younger, she knew what I was going to say before I said it. But there was something I had been holding onto for many years and I wanted to get it off my chest before it was too late. If not now, I would never get another opportunity. She would understand even if she couldn't hear me. In the past I could always talk to her and resolve any issue. This time I broached the subject in a roundabout fashion, not that she would be aware of it.

I said, "Hey, Beautiful! How yah feeling? I've been thinking a lot about the early days when Jo and I were kids back on 15th & Massachusetts. All the memories. I was a happy kid when we lived on 15th. Seems the time has just flown by. Can't believe how fast the years have gone by. Your hands feel soft. You been using that lotion that Joan sent you, huh. Now suddenly, I'm grown. Seems it was just yesterday I was scared to go out in the hall to the bathroom at night. But I had fun every day. My childhood was wonderful and exciting, all thanks to you. And most of my friends were right there in the neighborhood. I think back to my very earliest memories of 15th & Massachusetts and remember when Jo and I went to nursery school right across the street at the Stewart House. It was called the Delaney Nursery School. Jo and I had our own sleeping cots that folded up and stored away. And guess what-at some point much later in my life when I was working at the Stewart House, I saw those same sleeping cots stored away in an upstairs storage room. I remembered everything about that building, The Stewart House. I knew every passage and backroom in the place. I could hide in that building and never be found. And remember when we used to go visit your mother in Blue Island? It was like going to the farm. In fact, it was a farm. I remember that outhouse! Yeah! Remember when Jo tried to burn down the outhouse!! Jo said Grandma was so mad at her that when she finished braiding Jo's hair, Jo said she looked like a black Asian because her hair had been braided so tightly that her eyes were slits. Grandma used to go out in the yard and catch two chickens. Remember? Then she rang their necks at the same time, one bird in each hand. You could hear their necks popping. Then we'd have those same chickens for dinner. Talk about fresh chicken. Going to the well to get water was no fun either but we did it. We had fun running through the big fields. Yeah, Blue Island was a trip. I got hooked on chocolate milk at the elementary school in Blue Island.

"Oh, yeah, you always laughed when you talked about me as a toddler. I remember my milk bottle was a small Coca-Cola bottle; it was heavy and it would not break. I dropped it many times but it never even cracked. You were laughing so hard when you told me that one day I got mad about something and threw my bottle down hard on the floor. The problem was that the bottle landed on my foot before it hit the floor. You said I screamed for a few minutes, more out of frustration than pain and then I moved on. Apparently, it was no big deal. Some weeks later you said that for whatever reason, I was about go ballistic again, raising my bottle to slam it down to the floor, But suddenly I stopped in mid-action, with the Coke bottle high in the air and slowly and deliberately sat the bottle on the floor and then commenced to go tantrum. You told that to all the grownups and for years as I grew up, I remember them laughing about it. I do remember that Coke bottle-Buster. Oh, and the oatmeal for me and Jo every morning before we went to school. Didn't realize until I was a grownup that you were doing a very good job of being a mother. I thank you for everything you did for me. You were a good mom and I loved you like crazy. At one time, I thought that if you disappeared or died, I did not know what I would do. It was the worst thing that I could imagine. What made you even more special was that you were pretty. I knew that my friends who came to visit, didn't come to see me. They came to see you because you had big legs. Yeah, you did.

"What I really want to talk to you about is something that has been on my mind for a long time, many years, sixty-five years maybe in fact. All my life I have been trying to find it in my heart to forgive you for a pain you inflicted on me one day. That pain was almost unbearable. It was like I had a dagger driven into my heart. Frankly, I am surprised and thankful that I survived it all. You were at the very center of it all. It was like yesterday. Whenever life makes a turn on me, I remember the pain I suffered that day. I was convinced on that day that you did not love me anymore because if you did you would not have done that to me. Right now, as I speak, I can feel my emotions rising, my throat getting tighter. The pain is still there and today I wanted to end the pain and forgive you. Do you want to hear about it?

"Ok, it was June 1952. I was eleven. Jo was twelve. It was a bright sunny Sunday afternoon. The custom in the neighborhood was that on Sunday afternoons, after Sunday school and church, all the kids either went to the roller rink, the movies, or a carnival if one was in town. Nobody stayed home on Sunday afternoon. Nobody. That was just the way things were. That was the tradition. Carnivals were always setup two blocks down the street in the big vacant field. But first, we all had to go Sunday school and then put money in the collection plate during church services. I thought both were a complete waste of time-and money. Anyway, I keep getting off track. Oh, yeah. It was a bright beautiful Sunday. I was having a rough day at Sunday school. The lesson was on Genesis, the first book of the Bible and the story of Adam and Eve. Mr. Taylor was our teacher and he kept saying that Adam and Eve were the first people, and that Eve was born of Adam's ribs. Now, Ma, you know I had a problem with that! But I didn't say anything. He just kept talking, saying what I thought was some dumb shit. I listened as he went on about the apple and the serpent. To be clear, it was a serpent; it was a talking snake! Adam and Eve were warned not to have sex, but they did the nasty anyway. What would most guys do if they found themselves naked with a hot chick, a virgin no less who is also naked-and who likes apples! Suddenly a huge rumbling voice comes down from the heavens and says, "Thou shall not fornicate!" You and I used to talk about this when I was in elementary school. What I loved about talks with you was that if you didn't know something you said so. That impressed me. Bet you didn't know that either, did you?

"Ok, back to my main point. After dinner that Sunday, when it was time to go skating or the movies, you told me that I could not go out. I heard you but I didn't hear you; in reality you could not have been talking to me cause what you said made no sense. Not going to the movies or skating on a Sunday did not fit into my concept of reality. My mind did not accept the clarity and simplicity of the statement, so I continued moving forward, changing clothes. All the kids were going to the *"Roosevelt"*. You know the Roosevelt Theater right there on 15th & Broadway. The new *Tarzan* flick, starring Johnny Weissmuller, King of the Jungle was on. It cost twelve cents to get into the theater. Jo and I were usually given fifty cents for the two of us. We could buy everything we wanted with it. Once we were inside, it didn't take long for us to find our friends. I could almost pick Richard's voice out of the cacophony of shouts and screams coming from the kids. We knew we were a little early because *Tarzan* hadn't started yet. And to make sure nothing got out of hand there was St. Louis, the big, black, old policeman who also served as the usher/guard/police, otherwise the bouncer. I do not think you ever met St. Louis, Ma. He was a big, very dark, older man who carried a big flashlight. St. Louis was mean-spirited, and he swore a lot. You could hear him screaming profanities across the theater if he saw someone out of order. Funny, now that I'm older, I see he wasn't mean. He was a protector of the children. If a beam from his flashlight lit you up more than once while a movie was on, you were gone. Once the movie started the entire theater got quiet. Looking back, I see that the*" Roosevelt"* served as a kind of safe, entertaining community center for the kids. We were noisy, but nobody ever got seriously out of control there. St. Louis wouldn't allow it. He would slowly patrol up one isle and down another. He was our guardian disciplinarian with a nasty bark. Of course, we did not realize that at the time. There were few if any adults in the show on Sundays when Tarzan was playing; the kids owned the theater.

I used to think about *Tarzan* a lot cause deep down inside, I didn't like him. Wasn't sure but something about the dude just was not right. Years later I realized why. He was a white guy going to Africa, into the bush and becomes King of the Jungle. A white man swinging on a vine through the jungle. I don't think so. And the African brothers in the movies always looked like savages. Many were shown with bones through their noses just to emphasize their savagery. And you know, what made it all so sad, was that we, little black kids were rooting for Tarzan! We were so brainwashed that we didn't even acknowledge our own humanity.

"I remember getting lumps in my throat when we sang the Star Bangled Banner in primary school. When the teacher told everybody to stand up, put our hands over our hearts and sing the Star-Spangled Banner, I felt excited and proud. The teacher taught us about the man, Frances Scott Keyes, who wrote the song. He was famous. He was rich. He was white and he hated black people. He thought all of us, black folks should be slaves. Bet you didn't know that did you? Ma, check this out. One of the verses of the Star-Spangled Banner was never included in the popular song that we still sing today. Check this out: *Their blood has wash'd out their foul footstep's pollution. No refuge could save the hireling and the slave from the terror of flight or the gloom of the grave, And the Star-Spangled Banner in triumph doth wave O'er the land of the free and the home of the brave."* That's saying: "you can run, nigger but you can't hide. I stopped getting that lump in my throat. See, ain't you proud of me. I got a good edubacation." Did I ever tell you about the time I held a bullet over the flame on the stove? We were living down on 15ᵗʰ & Massachusetts and I don't know how or why but Jo and I must have been home alone-not sure. But I had found a real bullet. I held it over the flame on the stove with a pair of pliers. After a few minutes, it exploded. I can still hear the ringing in my ears to this day.

"So, as I continued getting ready to go out, you said, "I told you that you're not going out!" I was stunned. My head was swimming. I was dizzy. Could this really be happening to me? Mr. Taylor must have told on me. Never told you this but I never liked Mr. Taylor. You told me that whatever my plans were for the evening to just forget about them. This could not be happening, I thought. The other kids would never understand. To have to stay home on Sunday afternoon was absolute cruel and unusual punishment. There was nothing to do at home on a Sunday. It wasn't like I had a computer or a game boy or an Iphone. I didn't even have a radio in my room. There was nothing to do! Nothing! The church music on the radio playing all day long, made the whole apartment feel gloomy and sad. It was maddening. It was a punishment worse than death. I made several futile attempts to explain but nothing I said made any difference. You summed up your stand on the matter when you repeated something I allegedly said in Sunday school. "Mr. Taylor told me that you said: "The President had his wife, the First Lady and Adam had Eve, the First Pussy!" I was done. I was so busted. I was deserving of the punishment. Nevertheless, I felt deeply wounded. It was almost physical pain. For the first time in my life that I could remember and appreciate, I was given an absolute "No". I even cried. But there's nothing to do! I was sad. I was angry. I was confused. I was in such pain that I cried myself to sleep. Hours later when I woke up, I was really pissed at myself for going to sleep. I had slept through it. But the pain never left. Ever since that day I've been pissed off at you-going on seventy years now. So, I decided that I'd get it off my chest while I was over here tonight. Now just 'cause you can't hear me don't mean I didn't tell you. I'm just glad I got that off my chest. I'm not pissed at you anymore. We cool.

"Oh, yeah, Joan told me a story about when we all went to Jamaica. It was you and Sputnik, Joan and me. You and Joan hung out together; Sputnik and I hung out on the beach all day drinking as much Red Stripe beer as possible and smokin' ganja. He was funny. Before we even landed on the island, he was asking about how we're gonna get some weed. I assured him that by the time we reach our hotel, I will have some ganja. It was his first visit to the island and had no idea how to acquire the goods. But I knew. When we reached the terminal, I knew to keep an eye open for some of the porters who by wink or suggestion had contraband to sell for the incoming tourists. One guy caught my eye and with the flip of his hand, showed me that he was holding some product. Without words, he held up fingers indicating his price and I nodded agreement. Without ever saying a word, we made the transaction quickly and smoothly. His package even included rolling papers which I thought would be a problem acquiring. Sputnik never knew the transaction had taken place. When we were alone in the hotel room, he inquired again about getting some weed. I said, "Hey, man, I already got the goods." He was amazed. "When did you get it? "he asked as I brought out the package. Then he asked me the dumbest question one could imagine. "How do you know the weed is any good?" I laughed and said, "Sput, that's like going to China and wondering if the rice is any good. I think one would have to work hard to find some poor ganja in Jamaica." I rolled us a nice joint and we went out onto the balcony and lit up. I gave the joint to him so that he could take the first hit. He took a couple of pulls, inhaled deeply then handed the joint back to me. I took my time enjoying the smell and taste of the weed when I realized that Sput had gone back into the room. I put the joint out; it was more than three quarters left. When I went back inside, my dear macho nephew was laid out on his back on the big bed with his eyes closed muttering: "wowwww! wowwww!" I laughed at him all day. It was very good weed.

"Then you and Joan flew to Kingston. The flight from Montego Bay to Kingston takes only about an hour on a small prop plane. It wouldn't be very cost effective to fly big jets on such short runs. Both the Montego Bay and Kingston airports are always busy, ushering in thousands of tourists every year. Joan had me laughin' so hard when she explained how you were so unhappy with about everything! Room too cheesy. Water too cold. Food too spicy. Drinks too sweet. On and on and on. She said you were getting on her last nerve. You two were going to Kingston to visit Joan's Aunt Mae. Joan said she worked hard on the trip to keep you happy but it was difficult. The trip to Kingston was a general success since Aunt Mae was such a gracious and understanding host. You admitted that you had a good time visiting the beautiful house that Aunt Mae lived in. You bragged about how beautiful her garden was and how magnificent, you said her flowers were. You were very impressed with the flora. By the time you were getting comfortable in Kingston, it was time to return to Montego Bay.

The Kingston airport was bustling. Busy, busy. You and Joan were directed to your plane and that's when things changed. It was a small, twin engine, six passenger plane. It was owned and flown by a small independent airline. Inside there were seats for four passengers and two pilots who sat directly in front of you, without any partition. You could tap the pilots on their shoulder. You were not happy. Now days we would call that plane what we call souped up cars, a 'hooptie." It was a twin engine hooptie. The seatbelts were thin and frayed but there was one for every passenger. Then the worse happened. Before takeoff, it started to rain. It was assumed that the flight would be cancelled. It wasn't. Joan said that as you two sat there with the plane shaking and trembling, you looked like a ghost. Then the takeoff. The plane started down the runways roaring and bumping until it was airborne. The plane bounced and bumped as it gained speed and altitude. The rain had gotten heavier, and the pilots looked as though they were having trouble seeing out of the front window. One pilot appeared to be wiping of the inside of the front windshield so that he could see. The flight was turbulent as you gripped your seat and began praying. Joan said she tried to console you: "Grannie, it's ok. It'll smooth out. We're gonna be ok." You shot back as you gripped your seat tighter: "Don't talk! Please don't talk!" Joan laughed as she said you were having a 'come to Jesus' moment. The entire flight back to Montego Bay was bumpy. Joan was relieved. You were ecstatic! Joan said that for the rest of the trip you were the nicest most considerate person she had ever met. She laughed at how that plane ride had made you humble and so very glad to be alive. We both laughed about your attitude check".

As I said that laughing to myself, I felt pressure on my hand. The pressure got stronger. I looked down and my mother was squeezing my hand. Her squeeze got strong enough for me to know that she was there. I turned to the nurse to get his attention. He stood up and walked over to the bed. He acknowledged that my mother was without a doubt, responding to me. When I looked at her face, she was smiling! Big smile! squeezing my hand even harder. Tears rolled down both sides of her face. The smile on her face came from the laughter that I know she was feeling inside. She was laughing at me. I felt like an ass, but my mother was laughing at me. I was embarrassed, I was crying, I was laughing I was blown away.

At 3:00 am on October 20, 2016, just hours after I left my mother's bedside, I got the call. Jo said that just minutes earlier, Mom had passed away peacefully- smiling.

04093262-00841283

Printed in the United States
by Baker & Taylor Publisher Services